To Stephie
You have the
way to
move me

Love,
Jonata

SCIOUSNESS

JONATHAN BRICKLIN, EDITOR

Eirini Press (Eirinipress.com)
510 Long Hill Rd., Guilford, CT 06437

This book is the first in a series on non-duality from a Western perspective.

"Sciousness and Con-sciousness: William James and the Prime Reality of Non-dual Experience" first appeared (in an abbreviated form) in *The Journal of Transpersonal Psychology*.

"The Notion of Consciousness" first appeared (in an earlier draft) in the *Journal of Consciousness Studies*.

Library of Congress Control Number: 2007923616
Sciousness/edited by Jonathan Bricklin — 2nd edition
Includes bibliographical references
ISBN 978-0-9799989-0-4

1. Bricklin, Jonathan

2. James, William

3. Flournoy, Theodore

4. Consciousness (Philosophy)

For Laura, Noa, and Quincey

Contents

Preface

"Instead . . . of the stream of thought being one of *con*-sciousness, 'thinking its own existence along with whatever else it thinks' . . . it might be better called a stream of *Scious*ness pure and simple, thinking objects of some of which it makes what it calls a 'Me,' and only aware of its 'pure' Self in an abstract, hypothetic or conceptual way. Each 'section' of the stream would then be a bit of sciousness or knowledge of this sort, including and contemplating its 'me' and its 'not-me' as objects which work out their drama together, but not yet including or contemplating its own subjective being."

— William James, *The Principles of Psychology*

Two years after writing his celebrated book about the varieties of other people's religious experiences, William James presented a variety of his own: the prime reality of non-dual experience. He had suggested this possibility as early as 1890, in his textbook, *The Principles of Psychology,* but he did not develop the possibility until two essays published in 1904: "Does 'Consciousness' Exist?" and "A World of Pure Experience." In those essays James challenged the scientific worldview of his day that had divided reality into objects and matter on one side, and subjects and consciousness on the other. When quantum physicists began issuing the same challenge a decade later, they discovered that James had prepared the way. Neils Bohr, in particular, found James "most wonderful."*

As the first modern-trained scientist to affirm the prime reality of non-dual experience, James has also prepared the way for Westerners today who seek to comprehend mainstream Eastern spiritual teachings — such as advaita, yoga, taoism, and zen — or the mystic sidestreams of our own culture — such as Parmenides, Plotinus, and Eckhart. The "father of American psychology," James saw the discipline as a pathway to the fundamental nature of consciousness. He left us a rich inheritance, one that has yet to be claimed.

Certainly most of James's contemporaries were baffled by his thesis, and even James himself wavered in his embrace of it. One colleague, however, who had a deep appreciation for James's radical insight was the psychologist Theodore Flournoy. His illuminating commentary concludes this volume. It is preceded by James's own landmark essays, as well as a few related excerpts from other of his writings.

Offered as an introduction is an expanded version of an essay written for the Centennial of

* Pais, A. (1991), *Neils Bohr's Times: In Physics, Philosophy, and Polity.* (New York: Oxford University Press).

James's manifesto on non-duality. A manifesto of non-dualism from another era: the *Hsin-Hsin-Ming* by the third Zen patriarch, Sosan, sets the stage.

I.

On Believing in Mind
(Hsin-Hsin-Ming)

by Seng-ts'an (Sosan), Third Zen Patriarch

It's not difficult to discover your Buddha Mind
But just don't try to search for it.
Cease accepting and rejecting possible places
Where you think it can be found
And it will appear before you.

Be warned! The slightest exercise of preference
Will open a gulf as wide and deep
as the space between heaven and earth.

If you want to encounter your Buddha Mind
Don't have opinions about anything.
Opinions produce argument
And contentiousness is a disease of the mind.

Plunge into the depths.
Stillness is deep.
There's nothing profound in shallow waters.

The Buddha Mind is perfect and it encompasses the
universe.
It lacks nothing and has nothing in excess.
If you think that you can choose between its parts
You'll miss its very essence.

Don't cling to externals, the opposite things,
the things that exist as relative.
Accept them all impartially
And you won't have to waste time in pointless
choosing.

Judgments and discriminations block the flow
and stir the passions.
They roil the mind that needs stillness and peace.
If you go from either-or, this and that,
or any of the countless opposites,
You'll miss the whole, the One.
Following an opposite you'll be led astray,
away from the balancing center.
How can you hope to gain the One?

To decide what is, is to determine what's not.
But determining what's not can occupy you
so that it becomes what is.
The more you talk and think, the farther away you get.
Cease talking and thinking and you'll find it
everywhere.

If you let all things return to their source, that's fine.
But if you stop to think that this is your goal
And that this is what success depends upon
And strive and strive instead of simply letting go,
You won't be doing Zen.
The moment that you start discriminating and
    preferring you miss the mark.
Seeking the real is a false view
    which should also be abandoned.
Just let go. Cease searching and choosing.
Decisions give rise to confusions
    and in confusion where can a mind go?
All the opposing pairs come from the One Great
    Buddha Mind.
Accept the pairs with gentle resignation.
The Buddha Mind stays calm and still,
Keep your mind within it and nothing can
    disturb you.
The harmless and the harmful cease to exist.
Subjects when disengaged from their objects vanish
Just as surely as objects,
When disengaged from their subjects, vanish too.
Each depends on the existence of the other.
Understand this duality and you'll see
that both issue from the Void of the Absolute.

The Ground of all Being contains all the opposites.
From the One, all things originate.

What a waste of time to choose between coarse
    and fine.
Since the Great Mind gives birth to all things,
Embrace them all and let your prejudices die.

To realize the Great Mind be neither hesitant
    nor eager.
If you try to grasp it, you'll cling to air
    and fall into the way of heretics.
Where is the Great Dao? Can you lay It down?
Will It stay or go?
Is It not everywhere waiting for you
    to unite your nature with Its nature
    and become as trouble free as It is?

Don't tire your mind by worrying about what is real
    and what isn't,
About what to accept and what to reject.
If you want to know the One,
let your senses experience what comes your way,
But don't be swayed and don't involve yourself in
    what comes.
The wise man acts without emotion
and seems not to be acting at all.
The ignorant man lets his emotions get involved.
The wise man knows that all things are part of
    the One.
The ignorant man sees differences everywhere.

All things are the same at their core
    but clinging to one and discarding another
Is living in illusion.
A mind is not a fit judge of itself.
It is prejudiced in its own favor or disfavor.
It cannot see anything objectively.

Bodhi is far beyond all notions of good and evil,
    beyond all the pairs of opposites.
Daydreams are illusions and flowers in the sky
    never bloom.
They are figments of the imagination
    and not worth your consideration.
Profit and Loss, right and wrong, coarse and fine.
Let them all go.
Stay awake. Keep your eyes open.
Your daydreams will disappear.
If you do not make judgments, everything will be
    exactly as it is supposed to be.

Deep is the Tathagata's wisdom,
Lofty and beyond all illusions.
This is the One to which all things return
provided you do not separate them,
keeping some and casting others away.
Where can you put them anyway?
All things are within the One.
There is no outside.

The Ultimate has no pattern, no duality,
and is never partial.
Trust in this. Keep your faith strong.
When you lay down all distinctions there's
    nothing left
but Mind that is now pure, that radiates wisdom,
and is never tired.

When Mind passes beyond discriminations
Thoughts and feelings cannot plumb its depths.
The state is absolute and free.
There is neither self nor other.
You will be aware only that you are part of the One.
Everything is inside and nothing is outside.

All wise men everywhere understand this.
This knowledge is beyond time, long or short,
This knowledge is eternal. It neither is nor is not.
Everywhere is here and the smallest equals the
    largest.
Space cannot confine anything.
The largest equals the smallest.
There are no boundaries, no within and without.
What is and what is not are the same,
For what is not is equal to what is.
If you do not awaken to this truth,
    do not worry yourself about it.
Just believe that your Buddha Mind is not divided,

That it accepts all without judgment.
Give no thoughts to words and speeches or pretty
    plans
The eternal has no present, past or future.

II.

Sciousness and Con-sciousness:
William James and the Prime Reality of
Non-Dual Experience

by Jonathan Bricklin

Sciousness

> *"The Witness"* — William James's handwritten anno-
> tation next to the word "sciousness" in his own copy
> of *The Principles of Psychology.*

It is widely believed in the West that consciousness implies a self; that to be conscious (literally, to
"know with") is to be a *self* that knows. But William
James, who devoted most of his life to the study of
consciousness, dismissed this belief outright, claiming it to be "a perfectly wanton assumption":

> . . . not the faintest shadow of reason exists for sup-
> posing it true. As well might I contend that I cannot
> dream without dreaming that I dream, swear without
> swearing that I swear, deny without denying that I

deny, as maintain that I cannot know without knowing that I know.

The self or "I" was many things for James: "a
noun of position, just like 'this' or 'here';"* a state of
"peculiar *internality* . . . possess[ing] the quality of
seeming to be active"; a feeling of *"some bodily process,
for the most part taking place within the head"*; "a uniform feeling of 'warmth'";† to name a few. What it
was *not*, however, was an abiding subject-substance
in which "phenomena inhere." Nor was it a ground or
condition of consciousness:

> I may have either acquaintance-with, or knowledge-
> about, an object O without thinking about myself at
> all. It suffices for this that I think O, and that it ex-
> ist. If, in addition to thinking O, I also think that I ex-
> ist and that I know O, well and good; I then know one
> more thing, a fact about O, of which I previously was
> unmindful. That, however, does not prevent me from
> having already known O a good deal. O *per se*, or O *plus*
> P, are as good objects of knowledge as O *plus me* is.

* Though "here" is mostly thought of as an adverb, it is also a noun, defined as
such in Webster's as "Immediacy in space, abstracted from the other qualities
and relations of the immediate experience."

† "The past and present selves compared," says James, "are the same just so far
as they are the same, and no farther. A uniform feeling of 'warmth' . . . pervades them all; and this is what gives them a generic unity, and makes them
the same in kind" (1890, p. 318).

Consciousness is always a form of knowing. Sometimes it is a knowing "pure and simple," without an accompanying sense of "I." Sometimes, "along with" whatever else is known, consciousness has a sense of its "own existence" as knower. James labeled consciousness-without-self *"scious*ness," and con-sciousness-with-self *"con*-sciousness." [*From hereon the term "consciousness" will encompass both "sciousness" and* con-*sciousness, referring to a moment which might be one or the other, or moments alternating between one and the other. In this more general sense, "consciousness" is synonymous with "awareness" and "experience."*]

The existence of both kinds of consciousness was evident to James not only from simple, try-at-home experiments, like his O plus P introspection above, but from more exotic experiments (not infrequently tried at home in 19th-century America): the taking of ether. A commonly noted side effect of this drug was the loss of the sense of "I" *without the loss of consciousness.** Thoreau likened it "to exist[ing] in your roots — like a tree in winter," and advised: "If you have an inclination to travel, take the ether. You go beyond the farthest star." In *The Principles,* James

---

* James Austin, in his magisterial *Zen and the Brain,* trivializes the use of ether to attain spiritual enlightenment by quoting one of Oliver Wendell Holmes's encounters with it: "A strong smell of turpentine pervades throughout" (Austin, p. 239). But Austin fails to add that Holmes himself was not satisfied with that result and tried again. Of that second effort Holmes wrote: "I felt...that I really had seen the secret of the universe....Put Jesus Christ into a Brahma press and that's what you will get" (Holmes, quoted by Blood, p. 231).

quotes the following account of such travel:

> During the syncope there is absolute psychic anni-
> hilation, the absence of all consciousness; then at the
> beginning of coming to, one has at a certain moment
> a vague, limitless, infinite feeling — a sense of *exis-
> tence in general* without the least trace of distinction
> between the me and the not-me.

To this non-dual experience with ether just before
"coming-to," James adds his own personal testimony:
". . . as it [the effect of the ether] vanishes I seem to
wake to a sense of my own existence as something
additional to what had previously been there."

An American mystic who profoundly influ-
enced James, Benjamin Paul Blood,* put this moment of coming-to from the ether state at the center
of his mystical vision. Blood called this moment the
"Adamic surprise," invoking Adam's state of awareness *prior* to his eating from the tree of knowledge:

> There is an invariable and reliable condition (or un-
> condition) ensuing about the instant of recall from
> anaesthetic stupor to "coming to," in which the genius
> of being is revealed. . . . No words may express the
> imposing certainty of the patient that he is realizing

---

* A debt James publicly acknowledged in his last published essay (1910b).

the primordial Adamic surprise of Life.

The serpent's sales pitch notwithstanding, Adam did not gain knowledge when he bit into the apple; he didn't discover fire, or how to graft a tree. The "knowledge" Adam gained was knowledge of *self*, which is not so much knowledge as *belief*. Under the influence of ether, the basis of this belief vanishes, returning only as one "comes to."

"Comes to" from what? Can black-outs (including dreamless sleep) be confirmed to be other than black-*ins* of which only the last moment of blackness before "coming-to" is remembered? What of Tibetan Yogis, for example, who remember more? "Taught to develop lucidity first in their dreams and then in their *nondream* sleep," they are able "to remain continuously aware twenty-four hours a day." They black-*in* to dreamless sleep, and know nothing of black-*outs*.

Does anyone else? After all, a first-person account of "absolute psychic annihilation" or "the absence of all consciousness" would be tantamount to a description of what does not, indeed *can*not exist: absolute nothingness. While it may be possible to experience or imagine the relative absence of anything, it is impossible to experience or imagine absolute nothingness or emptiness.* Blackness, silence, the abyss,

---

* This argument was first made by the most influential of the pre-Socratic philosophers, Parmenides. Generally reckoned as the first Western logician,

empty *space*, however large or small, are all relative nothingness, merely. "Absence of all consciousness," therefore, is a far more difficult inference to substantiate than an ongoing blackness, all but the last moment of which has been forgotten. *Con*-sciousness, not sciousness, is all that can be said to go out in these gaps; gaps which are no more gaps than "a joint in a bamboo is a break in the wood."

James held that "pure and simple" consciousness, without a "*self*-brand" — sciousness — was not only a reality, it was the *prime* reality. For sciousness is not *distilled from* the "dual constitution" of subject-object consciousness (*con*-sciousness), like oil might be from pigment, but rather a "dual constitution" is *added to* it.

When James first introduced "sciousness" as a possible prime reality in *The Principles*, he backed off with the warning that it "traverse[s] common-sense" — something he felt comfortable doing as a philosopher, but not as a textbook writer for a conservative scientific community. He allowed that he might return to a consideration of sciousness at the conclusion of the book, where he would "indulge in some metaphysical reflections," but it was not until two years later, in his conclusion to his abridged edition of *The Principles*, that he felt emboldened to do so:

Parmenides is now known to have been a Pholarchos, or "lair leader," who facilitated trance-state healings in caves. (See Kingsley.)

Neither common-sense, nor psychology so far as it has yet been written, has ever doubted that the states of consciousness which that science studies are immediate data of experience. "Things" have been doubted, but thoughts and feelings have never been doubted. The outer world, but never the inner world, has been denied. Everyone assumes that we have direct introspective acquaintance with our thinking activity as such, with our consciousness as something inward and contrasted with the outer objects which it knows. Yet I must confess that for my part I cannot feel sure of this conclusion. Whenever I try to become sensible of thinking activity as such, what I catch is some bodily fact, an impression coming from my brow, or head, or throat, or nose. It seems as if consciousness as an inner activity were rather a *postulate* than a sensibly given fact, the postulate, namely, of a *knower* as correlative to all this known; and as if "*scious*ness" might be a better word by which to describe it. But "sciousness postulated as a hypothesis" is practically a very different thing from "states of consciousness apprehended with infallible certainty by an inner sense." For one thing, it throws the question of *who the knower really is* wide open . . . .

Thirteen years later, writing solely as a philosopher, James returned to his "parenthetical digression" of sciousness that "contradict[ed] the fundamental

assumption of *every* philosophic school," openly em-
bracing it. James had founded a new school of philosophy, called "radical empiricism," and non-dual
sciousness was its starting-point. He even wrote a
note to himself to "apologize for my dualistic language, in the Principles." James did not continue
to use the *word* "sciousness" in these later essays on
radical empiricism, but the concept is clearly there as
the "plain, unqualified ... existence" he comes to call
"pure experience," where there is "no self-splitting ...
into consciousness and what the consciousness is of."
(In this essay "sciousness" and "pure experience" will
be used interchangeably and in combination.)

West Meets East: Sciousness and Zen

Ether experiences notwithstanding, James *theo-
rized* about pure experience sciousness more than he
described instances of it. Yet had he consulted D. T.
Suzuki, destined to become the foremost explainer
of Zen to the West, and employed at the time as a
translator by a philosopher friend of James, he might
have done otherwise. For while James claimed ignorance of Buddhism, his fundamental insight that *"to
know immediately . . . or intuitively, is for mental content and object to be identical"* explicates Zen monks'
attempts to communicate their satori. Take, for example, the following:

> When Fa-ch'ang was dying, a squirrel screeched on
> the roof. "It's just this," he says, "and nothing else."

A sound as startling (yet nonthreatening) as a squirrel screeching on the roof bursts *con*-sciousness into sciousness insofar as "no dualism of being represented and representing resides in the experience . . . ." All seeing, tasting, hearing, smelling, touching, thinking, imaging, feeling are reduced to the experience of that screech. If, say, you were watching TV when a squirrel screeched nearby, you could not describe the TV image that coincided with its onset. Likewise, when you bite into a particularly rich piece of chocolate you lose the sensation of how the chocolate feels in your hand; when you see a shooting star, you stop hearing the crickets; and when the answer to a question you have been puzzling over for weeks suddenly bursts into awareness, you lose complete contact with all external sensations.

Sciousness has what James calls a "*naif* immediacy," never knowable as such, but only in "retrospection." Zen tradition is filled with examples of such im•mediated* experience. Typical is the account of the 9th-century monk, Xiangyan. Having become frustrated by his efforts to understand Zen through reading, Xiangyan abandoned his studies altogether

---

* Turning the adjective into a participle, to directly contrast the participle "mediated."

for meditation; one day, hearing pebbles strike a clump of bamboo, he became enlightened. All such examples of one-pointed satori evoke the original enlightenment of the Buddha who, after years of self-torturing meditation, attained enlightenment all-of-a-sudden, in a moment of im•mediated sciousness. The moment occurred after an all-night meditation session under the Bodhi tree, when he "glanced at the planet Venus gleaming in the eastern sky."

The satori bliss of sciousness, or what the Zen tradition interchangeably calls "one thought-instant" (*ekaksana*) and "no-thought-instant" (*aksana*), contrasts sharply with the mild disturbance (from the Latin word *turba* meaning "commotion" or "mob") of ordinary experience. Ordinarily, thoughts or images come with what James calls a "staining, fringe, or halo of obscurely felt relation to masses of other imagery." In the wholemind of sciousness this fringe drops away. Whatever awareness there is, is full awareness. It is "pure *onsense!*" with no residue of self inhabiting the moment.

Suzuki, for his part, immediately saw the connection between James's pure experience and Zen, and introduced James's writings to his teacher Kitaro Nishida. Nishida not only directly appropriated James's analysis, but also his expression "pure experience" in seeking to translate the direct-experience satori upon which Zen is based.* Suzuki, too, appropriated the phrase "pure experience" to define "this most fundamental experience . . . beyond differentiation."

Non-dualism was well established in the two strands that wove into Zen: Buddhism and Taoism. Buddhists distinguished between dualistic knowledge — *vi·jna* (bifurcated knowing) — and non-dual knowledge — *pra·jna* (springing-up-knowing). So, too, dualistic perception — *sa·vi·kalpa* (with-bifurcated-thought construction) — was contrasted with non-dual perception — *nir·vi·kalpa* (without-bifurcated-thought construction). And as for Taoism, Chuang Tzu claimed non-dualism — "when 'self' and 'other' lose their contrariety" — to be "the very essence of Tao." Zen borrowed from these non-dual ontologies, but at the same time rejected any borrowed doctrines as the ultimate foundation for truth. Truth in Zen is confirmed by direct experience or not at all.

The British empirical tradition that James adhered to also confirmed its truths by direct experience. Berkeley used it in denying the independent reality of objects. Hume used it in denying the independent reality of subjects. When James used it to

---

* Suzuki also married a student of James, who helped him with his translations. For more about the relationship between James, Nishida, and Suzuki, as well as reasons to suspect James exaggerated his ignorance of Buddhism, see Taylor, 1995.

confirm what was left, his own tradition converged with Zen. For Zen's "suchness" or "this-as-it-is-ness" is James's pure experience sciousness: "immediate experience in its passing," "a simple *that*" before it is "doubl[ed]" into

1. "a state of mind"
   and
2. "a reality intended thereby."

James's Koan

Common-sense says that mind and matter are distinct. Common-sense says that exterior material objects interact with *in*terior consciousness, and that such objects can survive the extinction not only of the subjects who behold them, but of consciousness itself. But if the experience of sciousness is the "always 'truth'" prime reality that James, in agreement with Zen, claims it to be, then consciousness is not *of* something (internalized), but *as* something (neither internalized nor externalized). Echoing the great Koan tradition of Zen, James delivers this world-shattering wisdom in the form of a question:

How, if "subject" and "object" were separated "by the whole diameter of being," and had no attributes in common, could it be so hard to tell, in a presented

and recognized material object, what part comes in
through the sense-organs and what part comes "out of
one's own head?"

There is a useful distinction to be drawn between
an object and a mere thought of an object. As James
put it, "Mental knives may be sharp, but they won't
cut real wood." Mere thoughts of objects are intan-
gible, internal, and inconsequential. "Real" (by-con-
trast-to-merely-mental) objects are tangible, external,
and consequential. Kicking a rock is one way to make
the distinction between a mental and a "real" object.
It is not, however, as Samuel Johnson believed, a
way to establish the independent existence of objects
themselves. For the touch of his foot on the rock, as
James's koan could have helped him understand, did
not confirm a realm beyond perception. What part
of the touch came in from the rock? What part came
out of his own head?

If full attention, unimpeded by expectation and
uninterrupted by emotional reaction, is given to
the contact of foot-touching-rock, its external hard
"objectness" is clearly realized to be an *aspect* of
consciousness. There is no prime reality of matter.
"'Matter,' as something *behind* physical phenomena,"
is merely a "postulate" of thought. Touch, however,
such as the first feel of sand between your toes, or
a friend's hand on your shoulder, or a Zen master's

thwack with a stick, readily manifests as the prime reality of im•mediated sciousness. "If a man has experienced the inexpressible," Johnson once remarked, "he is under no obligation to attempt to express it." He might, however, feel obligated to rethink fundamental assumptions about expressible experience, such as the absolute discrimination between subjects and objects. Had Johnson himself, with his kick, not been preoccupied with trying to distinguish mind from matter, the first touch of his foot on the rock might have dispelled the twin illusion on which the distinction is based: an internal *consciousness-without-object* and an external *object-without-consciousness.**

Flickering Self of Con-sciousness

While the undifferentiation of subject and object eludes expression, it does not elude experience. Not only does the sense of "I" not brand our every waking moment, it flickers in and out — a flickering that happens so rapidly that the transition from *con*-sciousness to sciousness and back to *con*-sciousness barely registers. The sense of "I" flickers out, for example, with a red flash at the window; it flickers back in when the red flash "becomes" a cardinal. Like

---

* "If the notions of subject and object are both the separate objects of consciousness, neither term has any real significance. An object, in the absence of a subject, cannot be what is normally called an object; and the subject, in the absence of an object, cannot be what is normally called the subject" (Levy, pp. 66-67).

the screech of the squirrel, the sensation of redness, when it first appears, is undefined, unconnected to anything else, unpositioned, without context; and if attention is without definition, position, or context, the sense of "I" is without definition, position or context, which is another way of saying it is no sense of "I" at all. The conversion of the red flash into a cardinal is the reconstitution of the sense of self.*

It is not that names or words always contextualize consciousness. If, for example, after identifying the red flash as a bird, I struggled to remember the name of the bird, the first moment of remembrance might feel as absent of context and self as the initial burst of red color; for a moment it would command full attention. But when it follows immediately upon the one-pointed sensation of redness, the word-thought for the redness, "cardinal," dis-tracts ("pulls apart") the one-pointed sensation of redness into two points:

1. a state of mind
2. a reality intended thereby.

The loss of the sense of "I" in a one-pointed,

---

* At the 2006 Tucson Toward a Science of Consciousness Conference, the philosopher who wrote the consciousness entry for the online *Stanford Encyclopedia of Philosophy* tried to give the audience a prime experience of consciousness by exhorting them to "Look at your hands!" But the presumption of subject and object was built into the command. Try instead the following: "Look!" A prime reality of sciousness comes first, before the subject-object consciousness supervenes.

wholemind moment of sciousness is not to be confused with feeling lost or disoriented. As James says,
when you are lost in a forest and say "Where am I?,"
that is the wrong question. You know where *you* are;
you don't know where everything else is. So, too,
when a red flash appears outside the window, the "I"
sense, oriented in thoughts and feelings of the past
and future, drops out in the wonderment of the present moment; but there is no feeling of being lost,
since there is no sense of a somewhere else to be.

In the moment just prior to a wholemind moment
of sciousness, however, there may be a sense of dis-
orientation, as whatever context had positioned the
"I" (the "everything else" of the forest wanderer) lin-
gers. If, say, I am sitting at my desk daydreaming, my
"I" positioned within the narrative of that dream, the
sudden absence of that narrative, and all its positioning images, in the first moment of the red flash outside my window, may be palpable. Like forest wan-
derers who feel lost, not because of where they *are*,
but because of where they are *not*, there is a palpable
presence of an absence.*

But most of the time the sense of self flickers out
and in so rapidly that its absence is not noticed. Black-
ins and recalls from dreamless sleep notwithstanding,

---

* The palpable presence of an absence, such as the "presence" of one's missing
car in the parking space from which it has been stolen or towed, has been
aptly described by Sartre in *Being and Nothingness*.

consciousness seems to be a continuous self-narrative, just as a rapid succession of film frames projected on a screen seems to be one uninterrupted narrative. But whenever we become *completely* absorbed in anything — such as a sunrise (just before the response "How beautiful!"), or dancing (when "the dancer becomes the dance") — that self-narrative is interrupted. "To forget the self," says the 12th-century Zen Master Dogen, "is to be actualized by myriad things."

Pre-assembled Thoughts

"If we could say in English 'it thinks,' as we say 'it rains' or 'it blows,' we should be stating the fact most simply and with the minimum of assumption." — William James

The very awareness of myriad moments seems to entail a unifying agency. How else could myriad moments be thought or felt in relationship to each other, including that most minimal relationship: difference? Even individual moments, including wholemind moments of sciousness, are made up of myriad details that seem to presuppose an organiz*er*, or, at the very least, an organiz*ing*. Does not any image or thought of more than one detail — that is, any image other than, perhaps, a monolithically perceived patch of color — entail "a manifold of coexisting ideas" that must be assembled? As James puts it:

If . . . the thought be "the pack of cards is on the table," we say "Well, isn't it a thought of the pack of cards? Isn't it of the cards as included in the pack? Isn't it of the table? And of the legs of the table as well? The table has legs — how can you think the table without virtually thinking its legs? Hasn't our thought, then, all these parts — one part for the pack and another for the table? And within the pack-part a part for each card, as within the table-part a part for each leg? And isn't each of these parts an idea? And can our thought, then, be anything but an assemblage or pack of ideas, each answering to some element of what it knows?"

But having made the argument for a manifold of coexisting ideas in any thought of more than a single detail, James immediately dismisses it, claiming that "not one of these assumptions is true." To make them is to commit a basic error: confusing a thought with what the thought "can be developed into." Although the thought of the pack of cards on the table is a thought about both "the pack of cards" and the "table," the "conscious constitution" of the thought is not one of plurality but of unity. As a whole unit unto itself it is an "entirely different subjective phenomenon" than the thought "the pack of cards" or "the table." Emphasizing the point with italics, James declares: *Whatever things are thought in relation are thought from the outset in a unity, in a single pulse of subjectivity, a single psychosis, feeling, or state of mind."*

No moment of consciousness, however complex, is to be confused with what it can later be broken down into. A stab of pain in a tooth, for instance, is not an accretion of different experiences, even if it can later be described as such. So, too, a simple thought, such as "table" (or "cards on table"), does not arise disassembled, like mail-order furniture, requiring assembly from an "I." It arrives whole. The more complex the relations within a single thought, the more its pre-assembled quality is manifest.

In saying that "things thought in relation are thought *from the outset* in a unity," James is making no claim as to *how* such unity is accomplished. The "how" of such unity remains a mystery — a mystery, he points out, that cannot "be made lighter" by assuming that it happens "inside the mind." To say, as some philosophers do, that a thought is unified "inside the mind," is to assume that there is something *un*unified outside the mind, a "chaotic manifold" that needs to be "reduced to order." The most renowned of these philosophers, Kant, called this chaotic manifold "noumena," or objects as they exist in themselves, without the admixture of thought; he then posited a "transcendental I," a *pure* "I," which, though never actually experienced in any way, must still exist in order to convert noumena into recognizable phenomena.* In place of the direct experience of an existing unity in thought, Kant thus posited two *un*experienced *concepts*. For James, however, Kant's description of "the facts" was "mythological," and his transcendental "I" (not to be confused with the empirical "me" of a sensed "I") "as ineffectual and windy an abortion as Philosophy can show." As James rightly observes, there is no evidence that thoughts come from unknown elements, brought together in an "internal machine-shop" in the mind:

> Experiences come on an enormous scale, and if we take them all together, they come in a chaos of incommensurable relations that we can not straighten out. We have to abstract different groups of them, and handle these separately if we are to talk of them at all. But how the experiences ever *get themselves made,* or *why* their characters and relations are just such as they appear, we can not begin to understand.

Still, even if there is no chaos of *un*known elements to bring into the known, the presumption persists that *known* elements brought into a relation with each other require a rela*tor* of some sort. How else to account for a unity formed not "from the out-

---

* About this conversion, James says "Although Kant's name for it — the 'original transcendental synthetic Unity of Apperception' — is so long, our consciousness about it is, according to him, short enough."

set" but in time? James's example of the pack of cards
on the table, for instance, is presented as a sentence:
"The pack of cards is on the table." While the up-
shot of this sentence is indeed a unified whole, and
such a unity, when it occurs at the end of the sentence, occurs "all at once," the parts are, nonetheless,
articulated temporally. Is temporal relating possible
without a rela*tor*? Mozart, in the act of composing a
sonata, claims to have heard the complete sonata "all
at once," in a "single glance of the mind," but most
of us need time to get from "twinkle" to "star." The
simplest melody (like the simplest sentence), whatever its ultimate unity, unfolds as a *succession*. There
may not be "a constant 'self' moving through successive experiences," but any experience of succession (as
opposed to an "all at once" "single glance") seems to
entail if not an assembler, at least something more
than the assembling itself. But does it?

James at Basho's Pond

> *"Succession is the thing."* Xenos Clark, in a letter to
> Benjamin Paul Blood, that Blood shared with James,
> defining the essence of "the anesthetic revelation."

When we hear a melody, do the earlier notes
hang around until they are pieced together with the
later notes, or is the cumulating experience newly re-

configured in each occurrent moment? What of the various thoughts of a poem read? Who or *what* links them together?

Take the famous haiku poem of Basho:

Old pond!
Frog jumps in
Sound of water

The three lines are distinct but cumulative: the second line building on the first, the third on the first two. Three different thoughts, one successive experience. But the successive experience of whom? The poet Basho? On the basis of these three lines we have not the slightest inkling who that might be. The creator of a delightful poem, surely, but the delight is derived from a total vacuuming out of subjective traces. The relating of this scene, in both its parts and its totality, does not depict the history of a subject in whom the experience inheres so much as the impersonal modifications of experience itself. There is no question that the three moments of the experience are related to each other. The question is, how are they related? A daughter, for example, is, at the same time, both related to her mother and independent of her. She has features that can be *traced back to* her mother, but these features reside in her now, completely independently of their source; there is no unifying agency relating each to the other.

So, too, the relationship between the lines in Basho's poem exists independently of any unifying agency. The "in" of the second line has inherited its meaning from the "pond" of the line before it. In one sense, then, the first line lives in the second line. But that inheritance of meaning in the second line does not imply the continued existence of the first line any more than the hair color that the daughter has inherited from her mother implies that the mother is still alive. The second line *as* written, and *if* read in the spirit in which it is written, is a new moment in a stream of sciousness, even if it contains something of a moment that came before it.

Granted it may take much meditation practice to even glimpse this spirit, in which everything that arises commands undivided attention upon arrival and then vanishes as the next point of focus arrives; and ultimately, perhaps, grace, to inhabit it fully. As the considered-to-be-enlightened Zen patriarch Huang Po mused about his students: "Why do they not copy me by letting each thought go as though it were nothing, or as though it were a piece of rotten wood, a stone, or the cold ashes of a dead fire?" Why indeed? But even from the vantage point of ordinary experience, where each moment of thought is not let go of before the next arrives, relationships between sequential moments are less artificially assigned to the moments themselves than to a go-between unifier.

Take, as James does, by way of illustration, the simplest of sequences — one letter of the alphabet followed by the next. The letter "m" comes before the letter "n," and "n" comes after "m"; but that does not imply that a before-after relationship exists *in-between* the two letters, actively linking them. The transitioning between two moments may be pro-tracted enough to suggest such active linking is tak-ing place; but whatever transitioning is experienced is, in fact, its own distinct moment in the sequence.* The distinction of such transitional moments is eas-ily overlooked, which is why James says "we ought to say a feeling of *and,* a feeling of *if,* a feeling of *but,* and a feeling of *by,* quite as readily as we say a feeling of *blue* and *cold.*" But with or without such distinct transitional thoughts as "and" or "is followed by," the thought "n" does not require the lingering presence of the thought "m" to assume its sequential sense. On the contrary, sequential sense, as James says, comes ready-made as its own distinct pulse:

> [I]f the plain facts be admitted ... the *pure* idea of *"n" is never in the mind at all,* when *"m"* has once gone be-fore; and . . . the feeling *"n-different-from-m"* is itself

* James likens such transitions to "flights of a bird" in-between "perchings."

an absolutely unique pulse of thought.

To believe that the experience of succession entails distinct, lingering moments that are actively unified is to confuse thought *in* succession with a thought *about* succession. As the psychologist Alfred Wilhelm Volkmann says, in a passage quoted by James, "The thinking of the sequence of B upon A is *another kind of thinking* from that which brought forth A and then brought forth B." Or, saying the same thing in different words: ". . . successive ideas are not yet the idea of succession, because succession *in* thought is not the thought *of* succession."* Succession *in* thought is what Kant called "bare succession," an unreflected-upon "vanishing and recommencing" of thoughts. Thought *of* succession, by contrast, is a *conceptualization* of this vanishing and recommencing. In this conceptualization, the otherwise unreflected-upon transition between different moments is abstracted into still points of thought, spread out in an imaginary row.

But in contrast to a thought *of* succession, thought *in* succession requires no such row of imaginary segments spread before and after an imaginarily contemporaneous "I." Instead of an "I," "'combining' or

* Any pre-known sequence, such as the alphabet, is, as it plays out, actually both at once: a thought in and of succession. "N-different-from-m" may be an "absolutely unique pulse of thought" but it is not an unanticipated thought, such as "n-different-from-w."

'synthesizing' two ideas [m and n]," there is a *single* "pulse of thought knowing two facts." Even Kant, in a self-sabotaging footnote, acknowledged as much:

> An elastic ball which impinges on another similar ball in a straight line communicates to the latter its whole motion, and therefore its whole state (that is, if we take account only of the positions in space). If, then, in analogy with such bodies, we postulate substances such that the one communicates to the other representations together with the consciousness of them, we can conceive a whole series of substances of which the first transmits its state together with its consciousness to the second, the second its own state with that of the preceding substance to the third, and this in turn the states of all the preceding substances together with its own consciousness and with their consciousness to another. The last substance would then be conscious of all the states of the previously changed substances, as being its own states, because they would have been transferred to it together with the consciousness of them. And yet it would not have been one and the same person in all these states.

What Kant believed to be possible, James claimed as actual. Introducing Kant's metaphor into *The Principles*, James held that "it is a patent fact of consciousness that a transmission like this actually occurs"; one thought does indeed pass into another without the mediation of an "I." Capitalizing the word "thought" to mean "the present mental state," James writes:

> Each pulse of cognitive consciousness, each Thought, dies away and is replaced by another. . . . Each later Thought, knowing and including thus the Thoughts which went before, is the final receptacle — and appropriating them is the final owner — of all that they contain and own. Each Thought is thus born an owner, and dies owned, transmitting whatever it realized as its self to its own later proprietor.

It reads like a commentary on Basho's poem.

If it does not read like an account of ordinary experience it is because ordinary experience assumes more than the impersonal arising of a "sequence of differents." Ordinary experience assumes a thinker generating and connecting passing thoughts, rather than the only "directly verifiable existent" — "the passing Thought itself."

The Gap Between Thoughts

> *"Many years ago, I was working with Nisargadatta Ma-haraj, an Indian teacher. He asked a woman who was au-dio taping for a new book, 'What will be the name of my next book?'* She replied, 'Beyond Consciousness.' *He said, 'No,* Prior *to Consciousness. Find out who you are* prior *to your last thought and stay there.'"* — Stephen Wolinsky

In the absence of distraction in which every moment is experienced as "a one thought-instant," the discontinuity between each thought-instant is not filled by a self, but a gap. James had introspected experience into "small enough pulses" to realize that the discontinuity between passing thoughts is mediated by the passing thoughts themselves. The "minimal fact" of experience, for James, was a 'passing' moment experienced as difference. Had his introspection deepened into even smaller pulses, he might have realized one more minimal fact about passing, *differing* moments: they do not go "indissolubly" into each other, "with no dark spot" between them, but, rather, are separated by the very "darkness" "out of" which they come. In ordinary experience, the space between thoughts is so fleeting as to be an "apparition." In meditation, however, the apparition is real: "If you watch very carefully," says Krishnamurti, "you will see that, though the response, the movement of thought, seems so swift, there are gaps, there are intervals between thoughts. Between two thoughts there is a period of silence which is not related to the thought process." In Tibetan Buddhism, the gap has a special name: "bardo," literally "in between."*

Some formal practitioners of meditation have even tried to quantify the frequency of the movements in and out of thoughts: 6,460,000 such moments in 24 hours (an average of one arising moment per 13.3 milliseconds), according to the Buddhist Sarvaastivaadins; a sect of Chinese Buddhists puts it at one thought per 20 milliseconds. Obviously, such speeds include both thoughts and thought fragments. But as has been argued recently for visual consciousness, all movements of consciousness are derivable from moments: discrete "static snapshots," like a strip of movie film.

Exactly analogous with cinema, the conversion of moments into movement can, depending on the speed of the conversion, appear with or without gaps: as a lurching parade or a flowing stream. There might even be both a maximum and minimum speed limit for consciousness just as there are for movies. A movie runs at 24 frames per second; too much

---

* While this term is more familiar to Westerners as the Tibetan name for the state between death and rebirth, in Tibet it more fundamentally refers to what meditation reveals: "at the death of each moment there is a gap, a discontinuity, before the arising of the next."

faster creates a whirring blur. Individual visual perceptual moments also have a maximum speed limit: around a hundred milliseconds. Any visual stimulus that vanishes faster than that goes unnoticed, even as a blur. As for a minimum speed limit, just as film frames can melt if they became stalled in a projector for more than a few seconds, so, too, a particular moment of consciousness cannot hang around indefinitely. "Any content of consciousness," according to neuroscientist Ernst Pöppel, "has a survival time of only three seconds." Even a seemingly single content of consciousness, such as the visual perception of a motionless external object, can never endure as single, but only as repeated rebirths of awareness; for, as Bergson noted, "if a mental state ceased to vary, its duration would cease to flow."

James, who lived in the infant stages of cinema, weighed in on its limit as a metaphor for consciousness:

> . . . snap-shots taken, as by a kinetoscopic camera . . .
> insert[ed] in our revolving lantern . . . cannot explain
> . . . what makes any single phenomenon be or go —
> you merely dot out the path of appearances which it
> traverses. For you cannot make continuous being out
> of discontinuities . . . . The stages into which you ana-
> lyze a change are states, the change itself goes on be-
> tween them. It lies along their intervals, inhabits what

> your definition fails to gather up, and thus eludes con-
> ceptual explanation altogether.

Static images of film cannot, obviously, explain "what makes any single phenomenon ... go." They themselves have a projector's moving mechanism to explain why *they* go. No static images could ever explain "life in its original coming."

But what of life in its original *being*? That the entire *content* of consciousness, no less than the entire content of cinema, can be broken up into still images, separated by still intervals, is becoming increasingly evident, "gathering up" more of the "definition" of change than James realized. "We may find movies convincing," writes neurologist Oliver Sacks, summing up several recent studies of visual consciousness, "precisely because we ourselves break up time and reality much as a movie camera does, into discrete frames, which we then reassemble into an apparently continuous flow."

It is only because film (at 24 frames per second) runs within the range of our own ordinary waking beta brain-wave rhythm (14-30 pulsations, or "bursts of neural energy," per second) that we don't perceive the entirely static nature of its contents. If film is run at 16 frames per second there would be a flicker effect, and at 8 frames per second (corresponding to the lower threshold of our brain's alpha rhythms), it would have the disjointed flow of the nickelodeon. Slow it down to 5 frames per second (corresponding to the theta rhythm of monks in Zazen) and "the viewer could then begin to distinguish the separate still photographs out of which the illusion of motion is created." No wonder that

Old pond!
Frog jumps in
Sound of the water

sprung out of a culture of meditation, in which monks habitually enter this snapshot-followed-by-snapshot theta state of consciousness.

And beyond the 3-7 pulses per second of theta are the near cessation of pulses of delta (the state of deep sleep and much of the first year of infancy, but a state rarely accessed when conscious) where "all motion in what passes for the physical universe has dropped dead still."* The 16th-century Buddhist monk Han Shan apparently accessed this state immediately upon attaining enlightenment:

I got up from my meditation bed, prostrated myself

---

* Invariant mental states are, presumably, also repeated births of awareness, of maximum three-second durations. It is not time but mutability that appears frozen. The absence of outward perceived changes overwhelms the presence of the inward dynamic processing, creating the sense that time itself is standing still.

before the Buddha shrine and did not have the perception of anything in motion. I lifted the blind and stood in front of the stone steps. Suddenly the wind blew through the trees in the courtyard, and the air was filled with flying leaves which, however, looked motionless .... When I went to the back yard to make water, the urine seemed not to be running.

In the West today, such "standstills," showing that consciousness can be "brought to a halt, stopped dead, for substantial periods," is a state known mainly as pathology:

Once [writes Sacks] I was called to the ward because Mrs. Y [a post-encephalitic patient on the drug L-Dopa] had started a bath, and there was now a flood in the bathroom. I found her standing completely motionless in the middle of the flood.

She jumped when I touched her, and said, "What happened?"

"You tell me," I answered.

She said that she had started to run a bath for herself, and there was an inch of water in the tub . . . and then I touched her, and she suddenly realized that the tub must have run over and caused a flood. But she had been stuck, transfixed, at that perceptual moment when there was just an inch of water in the bath.

James was well aware of the varying speed — from still to blur — of consciousness; of how "discrimination of successions" could, under the influence of fatigue, illness, ecstasy, or drugs, "become finer-grained, so that we noted ten stages in a process where previously we only noted one . . . ." In hashish intoxication, for example,

> there is a curious increase in the apparent time-perspective. We utter a sentence, and ere the end is reached the beginning seems already to date from indefinitely long ago. We enter a short street, and it is as if we should never get to the end of it.

In other altered states the opposite effect is experienced: "processes seem to fade rapidly without the compensating increase in the subdivisibility of successions."

We now know that there is no absolute clock-time; there is only consensus time. Brain-damage, drugs, ecstasy, or space-travel at super-high speeds, breaks the consensus. For astronauts whizzing by earth, and those in altered states of consciousness sitting in chairs, the clocks on the walls run at different speeds than for the rest of us. For some patients with Parkinson's disease, for example, the clock on the wall seems to be going "exceptionally fast." For others the hands move slowly. Nor does it take abnormal (ab*consensus*) experiences to appreciate that time is a "patently artificial" "construction." As James wrote, well in advance of Einstein: "we assume for certain purposes one 'objective' Time that *aequabiliter fluit* [flows evenly], but we don't livingly believe in or realize any such equally-flowing time." What we realize are moments of varying duration, and movements discriminated into varying degrees of successive moments.

Con-sciousness as the Whirlpool of Sciousness

> "There is no internal self or soul within and independent of the body-mind. The individual body-mind is a modification or Play upon the infinite, All-Pervading, Transcendental Being. The body-mind itself, in its contraction or recoil from the universal pattern of relations, suggests or implies the subjective internal self or independent soul idea." — Da Free John

In a "non-regressive satori" state of sciousness, the movement between one thought and another (separated by a momentary gap) is experienced as a simple transition between one moment and the next, "a bare succession . . . always vanishing and recommencing." In ordinary *con*-sciousness, however, instead of the vanishing and recommencing of pulses of thoughts *in* succession, such as

> Old pond
> Frog jumps in
> Sound of the water

a thought *of* succession is present as well; each moment-movement of thought is experienced not as an "absolutely unique pulse," but as actively related to other thoughts. This active relationship, or what James calls "some shading or other of relation" or "inward coloring," may be as simple as a sense of conjunction:

> Old pond!
> And a frog jumps in
> And a sound of the water

or a more complex causal relationship:

> The old pond!
> Made a splash
> When a frog jumped in

In these altered examples, Basho's one-pointed sciousness *in* succession has been replaced by a *dis*-tracted *con*-sciousness *of* succession. A "self" no less than a frog has jumped in, just as it more obviously does whenever the sequence is emotionally charged:

Old pond!
Feels peaceful
What's that?!
Wow, a frog!
There goes the silence!

But however much thoughts may be distracted from sciousness into *con*-sciousness, there is no independent "I" holding the thoughts together, let alone generating them. James held that *all* aspects of the experience of self arose "*in* the stream of consciousness." It could, of course, hardly be otherwise, since his metaphor of the stream of consciousness (not to be confused with a merely haphazard flow of thoughts)* was seen by him to be all-encompassing. No experience exists outside the stream. Nonetheless, at the risk of straining James's metaphor, we might say that the stream of consciousness flows unimpeded only in the absence of contracted self-feeling, as in meditation, or in the suchness state exemplified by Basho's original:

Old pond!
Frog jumps in
Sound of the water

---

* As in the popular usage of the term after James.

and that contracted feelings of self are as much a disturbance *of* the stream as something *in* it — a disturbance rather like a whirlpool, a turning in on itself that creates a formation so distinct it seems separated from that which constitutes it. James himself suggests this possibility in his presentation of the passive model of attention, where he identified the feeling of effort, a contracted self-feeling, with "eddies" in the stream of thought.*

The sense of self as an apparently separate formation in a stream of sciousness, as sciousness turning in on itself, was vividly described by Suzuki's star pupil, Alan Watts. Traveling away from his sense of self by means of LSD, Watts, like the ether anattanauts of the 19th-century, wrote about what it felt like to return: "The ego is a kind of flip, a knowing of knowing, a fearing of fearing. It's a curlicue, an extra jazz to experience, a sort of double-take or reverberation, a dithering of consciousness which is the same as anxiety."

By this reckoning, the whirl of self-feeling *obscures* the arising nature of the impersonal thought process by effectively filling in the gap between one thought and another. Because the stream of consciousness is ordinarily felt *with* "I," it is presumed to be being maintained *by* "I." But no "I" accounts for the coher-

---

* James cannot and does not oppose this passive model on psychological grounds. His objections are ethical. See Bricklin.

ence between thoughts any more than it accounts for the coherence within a single thought. The unity of relations that exists in any given thought or between thoughts is a fact of experience behind which we cannot go. "If anyone," says James, "urge that I assign no *reason* why the successive passing thoughts should inherit each other's possessions . . . I reply that the reason, if there be any, must lie where all real reasons lie, in the total sense or meaning of the world."

James's conviction that sense or meaning is not generated by an "I" but *conveyed* by a passing thought, that the stream of consciousness creates the "I" (and not the other way around), aligns him squarely with the central thesis of Eastern non-dual traditions from Advaita to Zen: *Tat tvam asi,* "That thou art." As the non-dualist Shankara expressed it 1,000 years before James: "If you say that experience depends upon an experiencer, we reply that on our view the experience is itself the experiencer." James, for all his skepticism toward what he called the "monistic music" of Eastern religion, seems almost to be paraphrasing Shankara when he says: *"If the passing thought be the directly verifiable existent which no school has hitherto doubted it to be, then that thought is itself the thinker,* and psychology need not look beyond."

The Actual Nucleus of the Apparent Self

Of the many phrases Watts uses to describe the "something additional," turning-in-on-itself sense of "I," let us isolate the word "reverberation." This is the same word, as it turns out, that James used to describe the feeling of "I" when he introspected upon it with*out* the assistance of a drug. The word "reverberation," defined by Webster's as "to throw back (sound)," literally means "to beat again." Besides being a distraction of sciousness into *con*-sciousness, what *is* this "I" reverberation, this second beat, that accompanies most, but by no means all, states of consciousness? James's answer to this question begins, as usual, with introspection:

> First of all, I am aware of a constant play of further-
> ances and hindrances in my thinking, of checks and
> releases, tendencies which run with desire, and ten-
> dencies which run the other way. Among the matters
> I think of, some range themselves on the side of the
> thought's interests, while others play an unfriendly
> part thereto . . . .

The impersonal nature of this "constant play of furtherances and hindrances" corroborates what James believed to be the "it thinks," impersonal nature of the thought process. The "checks and releases" he describes do not issue from his self. He does not *make* the constant play in his thinking, he merely becomes "aware" of it. A thought (such as the thought to get out of bed) arises; subsequent thoughts may reinforce the thought ("range *themselves*" — like cattle without a cowboy) or obstruct it ("play an unfriendly part" — like directorless actors). For both such "furtherances and hindrances" the reference point is not a *self* interest but a (preceding) "*thought's* interest."

While most people, James asserted, would affirm that the "self of all the other selves" is the

> . . . *active* element in all consciousness; saying that whatever qualities a man's feelings may possess, or whatever content his thought may include, there is a spiritual something in him which seems to *go out* to meet these qualities and contents, whilst they seem to *come in* to be received by it,

and while James himself sought to affirm this active element through his defense of free will, the grounds of his defense were not based on what he ultimately knew, but on what he wanted to believe. No one, James reluctantly declared, could ever prove that the active "spiritual something" that gives or withholds assent to a thought was an "original force," that "*contributes* energy to the result."

Now it may seem that all desire, regardless of

whether it is "furthered" or "hindered," manifests contracted self-feeling. Indeed, desire is so identified with self that absence of desire is commonly equated with the absence of self. Socrates, for example, seems almost to be quoting his near contemporary, the Buddha, when he says "to have no wants is divine." In both East and West, the "peace that surpasseth all understanding" transcends all desire. But a distinction needs to be drawn between desiring and hankering, or craving. A desire for something *can* be experienced, in and of itself, as one-pointed, without the second beat "reverberation" of self-feeling. An often quoted maxim of Zen Buddhism is "When you're hungry, eat. When you're tired, sleep;" and the Buddha himself partook of both activities, for the same reason as everyone else: there was a felt impulse or desire to do so — a desire that presumably did not disrupt his one-pointed, moment-to-moment, enlightenment.

Even a furtherance or hindrance of a desire or "thought's interest" need not necessarily reverberate with contracted self-feeling. The deepening affirmations, for example, that accompany the experience of a favorite symphony or a piece of chocolate may diminish the sense of self to the point that we "lose ourselves" in the experience. So, too, we get "lost" in a thought to the extent that the subsequent thoughts "range themselves" without interruption "on the side of the [antecedent] thought's interests." And while hindrances of a thought's interest may not create such a loss-of-self scenario, they, too, do not necessarily emphasize or manifest self-feeling. The hindrance of a thought's interest may quite simply be its own, discrete, un-reverberated moment, not experienced as connected-through-a-sense-of-hindering to the moment before. The thought to stay in bed, for example, even if it followed and hindered the thought to get up, could so completely predominate consciousness, bringing with it a wholly renewed appreciation of the warmth and comfort therein, that the thought of getting up would vanish as quickly and completely as, say, a baseball batter's thought to pull the ball down the third base line, immediately after he has, instead, socked it into the right field bleachers.

Logically, one cannot both get out of bed and stay in bed. Logically, these two thoughts are opposed to each other. But no *emotion* of opposition between them need necessarily arise. It is even possible for one thought to continue to rotate with an opposing thought without any more feeling of opposition between them than is felt by a skier zigzagging down a hill — turning left one moment, right the next, and then left again. Most often, however, when a pair of opposing thoughts rotates one with the other, a *feeling* of opposition is there as well. The opposition of one and the other is felt *in* one and the other; it is *how* they are experienced.

In such felt relationships between two opposing thoughts, each turning-toward is experienced also as a turning-from; each turning-from is experienced also as a turning-toward. Either way, it is in this two-pointed connection of welcoming and opposing that James locates the origin of the feeling of self. Not simply "the *constant* play of furtherances and hindrances," but the *reciprocal* or mutual play. Picking up his description from where we left off:

> The *mutual* inconsistencies and agreements, reinforcements and obstructions, which obtain amongst these objective matters reverberate backwards and produce what seem to be incessant reactions of my spontaneity upon them, welcoming or opposing, appropriating or disowning, striving with or against, saying yes or no. This palpitating inward life is, in me, that central nucleus which I just tried to describe in terms that all men might use.

This "central nucleus," what James refers to as "the central nucleus of the Self," is the kind of nucleus that has become familiar to contemporary physics: a blur of movement. Otherwise, it is no nucleus at all. It has nothing recognizable as a core. James emphasizes its coreless nature by calling it a "palpitating inward life."

The Temporal Landscape of Self

His paradigm of free will gave one example of the systole and diastole of these palpitations, where the rotation of two contradictory desires (to get up or to stay in bed) produced a "mutual" relationship between them. The "play of furtherances and hindrances" expressed itself in his paradigm as feelings of "welcoming" or "opposing": a saying "yes" to one thought that is felt as a saying "no" to the other. This "palpitating inward life" of welcoming and opposing is found at the center of every "I"-feeling emotion — which is to say every emotion except the blissful non-"I" mystical state of one-pointed sciousness, a state with no reverberation of approval or opposition, but only a neutral "whatever is, is." "I"-feeling emotions always reverberate. The leap-in-the-air thrill of a victory (as in witnessing a game-winning home run) is felt as a lift from the downward pull of defeat. The let-down feeling of defeat (as when the ball is caught at the top of the wall) is a fall from the up-lift feeling of victory. The "opposing," "disowning," "striving against" of negative emotions (anger, fear, hatred, envy, disgust, etc.) is a "saying no" to a present moment because it is a "saying yes" to the moment that preceded it. The "welcoming," "appropriating," "striving with" of positive emotions (triumph, relief, comfort, etc.) is a "saying yes" to a present moment because it is a "saying no" to its preceding moment.

Take, for example, the negative emotion of anger, an emotion which strongly reverberates with a contracted feeling of self. If every moment of *consciousness* were a moment of sciousness, then anger would not arise when something contrary to a previous thought's interest arose. In such a non-"I" state you would not feel anger even if, say, returning to your parked car, you found its windshield had been smashed and the radio stolen. The thought of your intact car might be a vivid image as you are rounding the corner to where it is parked, but it would vanish the instant you saw the car itself. By contrast, without such a wholemind processing of each moment as it comes, a sense of "whatever is, is," the thought of your car being intact would linger, in *felt opposition to* the sight before you, an opposition that is experienced as anger. Anger is a "saying no," a "striving against" what is, because it is a "saying yes," a "striving for" what *was* but *is no more*.

The reverberation of "I"-feeling emotion created by a mutual incompatibility between two moments is not merely a reverberation in time. Given the timeless quality of being-fully-in-the-moment, without reference to past or future — and hence without the borders that make even the present recognizable as such — the reverberation of "I"-feeling is the construction *of* time: not as an abstract concept, but as a felt relation, a palpitation between two moments.

To the extent that time can be said to exist at all, past, present and future exist too. Of these three, says James, the present is "the darkest in the whole series," since "nothing can be known *about* it till it be dead and gone." The present that *is* known, the present "practically cognized," is, James held, a "specious present," "delusively given as being a time that intervenes between the past and the future." Such specious present, more than a point, or even a "knife blade," is "a saddle-back, with a certain breadth of its own on which we sit perched, and from which we look in two directions of time."

James believed that a non-specious present, without breadth, "*must* exist, but that it *does* exist can never be a fact of our immediate experience." But what of the prime reality of im•mediated experience itself? James's adversarial colleague F. H. Bradley also affirmed that ". . . presence is really the negation of time, and never can properly be given in the series;" but he dismissed only time from the present, not "content." Is there an experienceable non-"saddle-back" present that has "content" but no breadth? Is an onsense moment of im•mediated sciousness just such a timeless present, a present, said Blood, that "has no breadth, for if it had, that which we seek would be the middle of that breadth"?

Such im•mediated experience, however, need not

be accepted as actual in order to accept the "*duration-block*" present, coming from the past, headed toward the future, as specious. All moments (whether the present's "just past" "rearward portion," or its antici-pating forward portion; a recollection of riding a tri-cycle, or an image of one's projected funeral) can only actually exist as aspects of "now."* Of course, it is one thing to *understand* that past and future are aspects of the ever-present now and another thing to experi-ence them as such. And rather than being experi-enced as what they always are — now, *present* mo-ments — the past and the future are most commonly experienced as a pulling-apart, a distraction from the now into a temporal landscape of di-stances. This other-than-the-ever-present-now distracted *con*-sci-ousness is the "palpitating inward life" of self — a movement into time, away from timeless, "breadth-less" sciousness.

What makes sciousness breadthless is not merely the felt absence of temporal borders, but the absence of any "I" positioning "here" to which such borders can refer. "The past is nowhere," says physicist David Bohm. The future, too. But they exist as the imagi-

---

*Alan Watts relates the following conversation with his wife: "One evening, when Eleanor and I were walking home from a meditation session, I began to discuss the method of concentration on the eternal present. Whereupon she said, 'Why try to concentrate on it? What else is there to be aware of? Your memories are all in the present, just as much as the trees over there. Your thoughts about the future are also in the present . . . there's simply no way of getting out of it.' With that remark my whole sense of weight vanished. . . . You could have knocked me over with a feather."

nary temporal landscape that the "I" reverberates as.

We just saw one example of this temporal landscape. In anger, an inconsistency from one moment to the next is experienced as a mutual inconsistency that invokes, as much as it relates, two moments of time. This felt temporal relationship applies not only to open anger but to the myriad resentments and frustrations that palpitate more feebly throughout the day. A horn honks outside my study, breaking the silence that was there and, insofar as I am angry, is *still* there, an *imagined* there, in felt opposition to the sound of the horn. Whether it be the smallest ripple of frustration — such as from writing the wrong date on a check — or open rage — such as from discovering your spouse is having an affair — a relationship between past and present is activated. In all cases of anger, frustration, or resentment, the past is not simply recalled — as just another image in the ever-arising now — it is *revived*, to the point that the distracted "I" of *con*-sciousness seems to exist *between* two different moments of time, represented as different spaces within a temporal landscape.

The temporal landscaping of distracted *con*-sciousness applies as well to the other, primal negative emotion — fear. While the sense of self, the "palpitating inward life," that arises with anger palpitates between past and present, the sense of self that arises with fear palpitates between present and future. If, for example, while walking down a city street, I reach for my wallet and discover that it is not there, my initial response is not anger but fear. I stop dead in my tracks and gasp. My step, my very breath, is interrupted. Not the look back of "what happened?" but a look forward with "what *will* happen?" While anger is a striving against "what is" because it is a striving *for* "what was," fear is a striving against "what is" because it is a striving for "what will be." Thus cancer patients, racked with pain, full of the knowledge that they have only a few days to live, may face a gun (possibly their own) with less fear than those filled with thoughts of the future.* In all instances of fear, the sense of self that is threatened is a self of the future; in all instances of anger the sense of self that is threatened is a self of the past.† Both anger and fear are a lesson in what is actual as opposed to what is imagined; to the degree that we stay angry or fearful, the lesson hasn't been learned.

---

* Pain cannot be experienced as sciousness, as we have defined it, but there are many testimonies of transcending pain through transcending a feeling of self. Yogis and Christian martyrs alike could identify with the final sermon of the besieged 16th-century Zen abbot Kwaisen who, along with his fellow monks, was locked into a room that was then set on fire. Sitting cross-legged with them in front of the image of the Buddha, the abbot said: "For a peaceful meditation, we need not go to the mountains and streams. When thoughts are quieted down, fire itself is cool and refreshing." So, too, morphine's power over pain is not over the pain itself, but over the response to the pain. As the creator of the drug ecstasy, Alexander Shulgin, put it: "[Morphine] doesn't quiet the pain — it makes you indifferent to it. It depersonalizes the pain."

† Anger can involve the loss of a future scenario, but what fuels the anger is clinging to the sense of what the future *was* supposed to be.

Sciousness as Enlightenment

Given that the contractile emotions of anger and fear cannot be experienced in one-pointed sciousness, it is not surprising that accounts of enlightened persons, such as the Buddha, are absent instances of either emotion. In his *The Varieties of Religious Experience*, James quotes the following first-hand account from Richard Bucke's *Cosmic Consciousness*, depicting Bucke's mystical poet friend, Walt Whitman: ". . . he never spoke in anger and apparently never was angry. He never exhibited fear, and I do not believe he ever felt it."* While both anger and fear are commonly believed to focus attention, they are, in fact, always a sign that attention is, instead, distracted. As every accomplished martial artist knows, neither anger nor fear facilitates the moment-to-moment awareness required for self-defense. Indeed, the greater the absorption in the precise movement

---

* How cosmically conscious or enlightened Whitman remained throughout his lifetime is arguable. In his old age, however, he recalled the ecstatic state of his younger years, in which "the whole body is elevated to a state by others unknown — inwardly and outwardly illuminated, purified," and, in a "marvelous transformation from the old timorousness...[s]orrows and disappointments cease — there is no more borrowing trouble in advance...a man realizes the venerable myth — he is a god walking the earth...." If this testimony, corroborated, in part, by his friends and acquaintances, is not enough to convince us that Whitman did experience something like, if not equivalent to, the Buddha's enlightenment, there are the many photographs of the man (see, especially, the photograph Bucke called "the Christ likeness"), which confirm Whitman's own words about how "the marvelous transformation" altered his appearance: "A singular charm, more than beauty, flickers out of, and over, the face — a curious transparency beams in the eyes, both in the iris and the white. . . ." Such "transparency beams" appear to radiate out of our contemporary mystic, the "nowist," Eckhart Tolle.

of, say, a fist coming towards you, rather than in any feeling you might have about it, the greater the chance of avoiding it.

Nor is it only "negative" emotions that distract sciousness. If sciousness is an "infinite feeling" of blissful rapture, then no "positive" emotions can add to this rapture, but must, like negative emotions, distract from it. This is hardly surprising since, as we saw, "positive" emotions arise only in tandem with "negative" emotions. While it is true that bliss and rapture are also considered "positive" emotions, they are not felt as a response to, or in a relationship with, a non-blissful or negative emotion. Bliss and rapture are, instead, more like trap doors that drop us out of positive-negative duality altogether. The surprise scent of a rose, for instance, that comes out of no-where, is a blissful, non-"I" moment of sciousness, fundamentally different than the joy experienced from the scent of a rose sniffed to see if it has a scent. Unlike the blissful scent of a rose that wafts in by surprise, the "positive" feeling we get from the test sniff has an additional source: the allayment of a negative feeling (however slight) that it wouldn't have any smell. Although brief moments of bliss, *complete unto themselves,* may be more frequently experienced throughout the day than is commonly suspected, most "positive" feelings are not non-"I" moments of bliss, but are connected to feelings of striving for and against. And even a blissful moment, as it arises, may instantly turn into something to be striven for — its preservation — which is simultaneously a striving against its disappearance.

The reverberation of striving for and against, of welcoming and opposing, that generates the sense of self, defines a range within which all emotions arise. Every emotion is found somewhere between them. To focus, however, as James does, exclusively on the movement between the polar opposites of welcoming and opposing is to lose sight of a more fundamental movement: the movement between a neutral state of consciousness and all others — that is, the movement between sciousness and *con*-sciousness. To describe the feeling of self without reference to sciousness is like describing sound without silence — the silence that forms the contour of any sound that is heard. Just as there can be no sense of sound without a sense of silence, there can be no sense of self without a non-self background to give it definition. "The palpitating inward life" of welcoming and opposing cannot itself give rise to self-feeling any more than the change from soft to loud gives rise to sound. As sound is defined by its contrast to silence, so, too, the "reverberation" (second beat) of "I" is defined by its contrast to a first beat non-"I."

James's omission of neutral consciousness, or sciousness, from his depiction of the self of selves, is what leads him to the oxymoronic conclusion that the ". . . reinforcements and obstructions which obtain amongst . . . objective matters . . . produce what seem to be incessant reactions of my spontaneity ...." "*Produce* incessant reactions of my spontaneity?" Isn't the defining characteristic of spontaneity the very fact that no known source produces it? James was not witnessing incessantly produced reactions of his spontaneity; he was witnessing the incessant formation of an "I"-sense within the stream of sciousness — what Watts referred to as a "double take" and what they both termed a "reverberation." This "reverberation" is not an *activity* of self, but the *creation* of self.

The core of that creation — a palpitating inward life of mutually reciprocating feelings of welcoming and opposing — is what the Buddha lost, never to regain, on the day of his enlightenment. As he himself characterized it: "Having . . . abandoned favoring and opposing, whatever feeling he feels, whether pleasant or painful or whether neither-painful-or-pleasant." Such an enlightened state does not, as we said, entail the *complete* extinction of desire, as is sometimes (erroneously) attributed to it, but, rather, the absence of desire that any given moment be other than it turns out to be. It is the absence of such *hankering* desire in the Buddha, as in other mystics, which corroborates James's sense that "I" feeling is a by-product of the interplay between feelings of welcoming and opposing; for it is only in the *absence* of these feelings that the wholemind state arises. Like dancers who find themselves "in sync" with the beat of a drum, neither welcoming one beat over another, or wondering how to respond or how they appear to others, but existing with the beat, so that they have no sense of themselves as dancers but only a sense of dance, mystics have discovered that it is possible to just be with each passing moment, neither leaning toward it nor away from it, and having not the slightest sensation that *it* need be otherwise. In such a state, as Whitman says, every event, every encounter "is subdued into sustenance."

Such enlightened moment-to-moment con-sciousness, as exemplified by Whitman, was extolled by James in a talk he gave to students. But a few years later, in his *Varieties* lecture to professors, he turned critical. Ever the pragmatist, James claimed that Whitman's "mystic ontological emotion," free of "all contractile elements" "divert[s] our attention" from hardships, such as "disease and death." But James's pragmatism is misinformed here. Whitman, a medic during the Civil War, was no such diverter. His po-etry is filled with corpses and maggots:

> Behold this compost! behold it well!
> Perhaps every mite has once form'd part of a sick person
> — yet behold!

Indeed, it is precisely *because* Whitman's poetry is free of all contractile elements that diversion plays no part in it. Only in the enlightened state of pure-experience sciousness — uncompromised by welcoming and opposing — can one "behold well" every moment.

But if James misses the full practical value of such a state in his assessment of Whitman early in *The Varieties,* he compensates for it later by commending the example of the Christian mystic Catherine of Genoa, an example that can be taken as illustrating his epistemology as much as her spirituality:

> [S]he took cognizance of things, only as they were presented to her in succession, *moment by moment.*"
> To her holy soul, "the divine moment was the present moment, . . . and when the present moment was estimated in itself and in its relations, and when the duty that was involved in it was accomplished, it was permitted to pass away as if it had never been, and to give way to the facts and duties of the moment which came after.

James lamented that his own "constitution" shut him out from mystical experiences. He knew more than he realized.

References

Aitken, Robert (1978), A Zen Wave: Basho's Haiku and Zen (New York: Weatherhill).

Allen, Gay Wilson (1975), *The New Walt Whitman Handbook* (New York: New York University Press).

Austin, James H. (1998), *Zen and the Brain* (Cambridge, MA: MIT Press).

Bergson, Henri (1911/1944), *Creative Evolution* (New York: Random House).

Bhikkus Nanamoli & Bodhi (Trans.) (1995), *The Middle Length Discourses of the Buddha: A Translation of the Majjhima Nikaya* (Boston: Wisdom Publications).

Blood, Benjamin Paul (1920), *Pluriverse* (Boston: Marshall Jones Company).

Bohm, David (1994), *Thought as System* (New York: Routledge).

Bradley, F.H. (1883/1994), "The Principles of Logic," in Allard, James & Stock, Guy (Eds.), *Writings on Logic and Metaphysics* (New York: Oxford University Press).

Bricklin, J. (1999), "A Variety of Religious Experience: William James and the Non-Reality of Free Will," in Libet, Benjamin, Freeman, Anthony & Sutherland, Keith (Eds.), *The Volitional Brain: Towards a Neuroscience of Free Will* (UK: Imprint Academic).

Brown, Ethan (2002), "Professor X," *Wired*, **10** (9), 114-149.

Burkhardt, Frederick (1981), *The Works of William James: The Principles of Psychology*, Vol. III (Cambridge, MA: Harvard University Press).

Cleary, Thomas (2001), *Classics of Buddhism and Zen*, Vol. 4 (Boston: Shambhala).

Crick, F. & Koch, C. (2003), "A Framework for Consciousness," *Nature Neuroscience*, **6** (2), 119-126.

Eddy, Mary Baker (1906), *Science and Health* (Boston: A. V. Stewart).

Grof, Stanislav (1993), *The Holotropic Mind* (San Francisco: Harper Collins).

Hameroff, Stuart & Penrose, Roger (1996), "Conscious Events as Orchestrated Space-Time Selections," *Journal of Consciousness Studies*, **3** (1), 36-53.

Huang Po (9th - century AD/1958), *The Zen Teaching of Huang Po: On The Transmission of Mind* (trans. by John Blofeld) (New York: Grove).

James, William (1890/1983), *The Principles of Psychology* (Cambridge, MA: Harvard University Press).

James, William (1892/1992), *Psychology: The Briefer Course*, in *William James: Writings: 1878-1899* (New York: Library of America).

James, William (1894/1987), "The Knowing of Things Together," in *William James: Writings: 1878-1899* (New York: Library of America).

James, William (1897/1992), *The Will to Believe and Other Essays in Popular Philosophy*, in *William James: Writings: 1878-1899* (New York: Library of America).

James, William (1898/1992), "Human Immortality," in *William James: Writings: 1878-1899* (New York: Library of America).

James, William (1899/1992), *Talks to Teachers on Psychology and to Students on Some of Life's Ideals*, in *William James: Writings: 1878-1899* (New York: Library of America).

James, William (1902/1987), *The Varieties of Religious Experience*, in *William James: Writings 1902-1910* (New York: Library of America).

James, William (1904a/1987), "Does 'Consciousness' Exist?," in *William James: Writings 1902-1910* (New York: Library of America).

James, William (1904b/1987), "A World of Pure Experience," in *William James: Writings 1902-1910* (New York: Library of America).

James, William (1905/1987), "How Two Minds Can Know One Thing," in *William James: Writings 1902-1910* (New York: Library of America).

James, William (1909a/1987), *The Meaning of Truth: A Sequel to Pragmatism*, in *William James: Writings 1902-1910* (New York: Library of America).

James, William (1909b/1987), "A Pluralistic Mystic," in *William James: Writings 1902-1910* (New York: Library of America).

James, William (1910a/1987), "A Suggestion About Mysticism," in *William James: Writings 1902-1910* (New York: Library of America).

James, William (1910b/1987), "A Pluralistic Mystic," in *William James: Writings 1902-1910* (New York: Library of America).

James, William (1920), *The Letters of William James*, Vols. I-II (Boston: The Atlantic Monthly Press).

James, William (1988), *Manuscript Essays and Notes* (Cambridge, MA: Harvard University Press).

John, Da Free (1980), *Scientific Proof of the Existence of God Will Soon Be Announced by the White House* (Middletown, CA: The Dawn Horse Press).

Kant, Immanuel (1965), *Critique of Pure Reason* (New York: St. Martin's Press).

Kaplan, Justin (1980), *Walt Whitman, a Life* (New York: Simon and Schuster).

Kapleau, Philip (1965/1989), *The Three Pillars of Zen* (New York: Anchor Books).

Kasprow, Mark & Scotton, Bruce (1999), "A Review of Transpersonal Theory and its Application to the Practice of Psychotherapy," *The Journal of Psychotherapy Practice and Research*, 8 (1), 12-23.

Kingsley, Peter (1999), *In The Dark Places of Wisdom* (San Francisco: Golden Sufi Press).

Krishnamurti, J. (1954), *The First and Last Freedom* (New York: Harper and Row).

Lancaster, Brian (1991), *Mind, Brain and Human Potential* (Rockport, MA: Element Inc.).

Loy, David (1998), *Nonduality: A Study in Comparative Philosophy* (Amherst, NY: Humanity Books).

Lu K'uan Yü (1971), *Practical Buddhism* (London: Rider).

Pais, Abraham (1991), *Neils Bohr's Times* (New York: Clarendon Press).

Pöppel, Ernst (1988), *Mindworks: Time and Conscious Experience* (Boston: Harcourt Brace Jovanovich).

Ray, Reginald A. (2001), *Secret of the Vajra World: The Tantric Buddhism of Tibet* (Boston: Shambhala).

Sacks, Oliver (2004a), "In the River of Consciousness," *New York Review of Books*, January 15, 2004, http://www.nybooks.com/articles/17030.

Sacks, Oliver (2004b), "Speed: Alterations of Time and Movement," *New Yorker*, August 23, 2004.

Sartre, Jean-Paul (1956), *Being and Nothingness* (New York: Philosophical Library).

Shankara, Sri (1982), *"That Thou Art": Chapter XVIII of The Thousand Teachings (Upadesasahasri) of Sri Shankara* (trans. by Alston, A. J.) (London: Shanti Sadan).

Skrupskelis, Ignas & Berkeley, Elizabeth (1997), *The Correspondence of William James*, Vol. 5 (Charlottesville, VA: University of Virginia).

Suzuki, Daisetz T. (1954), "Zen and Pragmatism — A Reply (Comment and Discussion)," *Philosophy East and West*, 4 (2), 167-174.

Suzuki, Daisetz T. (1956), *Zen Buddhism: Selected Writings of D.T. Suzuki* (New York: Doubleday).

Suzuki, Daisetz T. (1959), *Zen and Japanese Culture* (Princeton, NJ: Princeton University Press).

Talbot, Michael (1991), *The Holographic Universe* (New York: Harper Collins).

Tanashi, Kazuaki (1985), *Moon in a Dewdrop: Writings of Zen Master Dogen* (San Francisco: Northpoint Press).

Taylor, Eugene (1995), "Swedenborgian Roots of American Pragmatism: The Case of D.T. Suzuki," *Studia Swedenborgiana*, 9 (2).

Taylor, Eugene (1996), "William James and Transpersonal Psychiatry," in Chinen, Allen, Scotton, Bruce & J. Battista, John (Eds.), *Textbook of Transpersonal Psychiatry and Psychology*, 21-27 (New York: Basic Books).

Thoreau, Henry David (1848-1851/1990), *Journal Vol. 3* (Princeton, NJ: Princeton University Press).

Walsh, Roger & Vaughan, Frances (1992), "Lucid dreaming: Some Transpersonal Implications," *Journal of Transpersonal Psychology*, 24 (2), 193-200.

Watts, Alan (1957), *The Way of Zen* (New York: Vintage/Random House).

Watts, Alan (1962), *The Joyous Cosmology* (New York: Vintage/Random House).

Watts, Alan (1973), *In My Own Way: An Autobiography* (New York: Vintage/Random House).

Wolinsky, Stephen (1993), *Quantum Consciousness* (Connecticut: Bramble Books).

Xenophon (4th-century/1923), "Memorabilea" in *Xenophon*, translated by Brownson, Todd, Marchant (New York: W. Heinemann; G.P. Putnam's Sons).

Notes

p. 19:   "The Witness": Burkhardt, Bowers & Skrupskelis, p. 1149.

p. 19:   It is widely believed in the West ...: For an excellent treatise on the fundamental importance of non-dual consciousness in the East, see Loy.

pp. 19-20: "a perfectly wanton assumption ... not the faintest shadow ... knowing that I know.": James, 1890, p. 264.

p. 20:   "a noun of position ... 'here'": James, 1909b, p. 803n.

p. 20:   "peculiar *internality* ... active": James, 1892, p. 179.

p. 20:   "a uniform feeling of 'warmth'": James, 1890, p. 287.

p. 20:   *not* ... an abiding subject-object ... "phenomena inhere.": *Ibid.*, p. 328.

p. 20:   "I may have either an acquaintance-with ... *me* is.": *Ibid.*, pp. 264-265.

p. 21:   "pure and simple": *Ibid.*, p. 290.

p. 21:   "along with" ... "own existence": *Ibid.*

p. 21:   James labeled consciousness-without-self ... "*con*-sciousness.": *Ibid.*

p. 21:   Thoreau likened it .... "farthest star.": Thoreau, p. 218.

p. 22:   "During the syncope ... not-me.": James, 1890, p. 263.

p. 22:   "... as it [the effect of the ether] vanishes ... been there.": *Ibid.*, p. 264.

p. 22:   "Adamic surprise": Blood, quoted by James, 1910b, p. 1306.

pp. 22-23: "There is an invariable and reliable condition ... of Life.": *Ibid.*: The last sentence, also quoted in an extended footnote in *The Varieties of Religious Experience*, p. 352, is attributed by Blood himself to fellow anaesthetic revelationist Xenos Clark, along with all but the last two paragraphs of passages that James attributes to Blood in that same footnote. See Blood, pp. 233, 235.

p. 23:   "Taught to develop lucidity first in their dreams ... a day.": Walsh & Vaughn, p. 198, emphasis added.

p. 24:   "a joint in the bamboo is a break in the wood.": James, 1890, Vol. I, p. 240. James used this bamboo joint analogy to describe the gap between the thought of one object and another.

p. 24:   "*self*-brand": James, 1890, p. 320. (Compare Brian Lancaster's term "'I'-tag", Lancaster, p. xii, and throughout.)

p. 24:   sciousness is not *distilled from* ... "dual constitution is *added to* it.": James, 1904a, p. 1144, 1151.

p. 24:   "traverse[s] common-sense": James, 1890, p. 291.

p. 24:   "indulge in some metaphysical reflections": "At the conclusion of the volume, however, I may permit myself to revert again to the doubts here provisionally mooted, and will indulge in some metaphysical reflections suggested by them." This sentence, which appears on p. 305 of the original *The Principles of Psychology*, was deleted from subsequent editions.

p. 25:   "Neither common-sense ... wide open": James, 1892, p. 467.

pp. 25-26: "parenthetical digression" ... "philosophic school": James, 1890, p. 291.

p. 26:   "apologize for my dualistic language in the Principles.": James, 1988, p. 29.

p. 26:   "plain, unqualified" ... "what the consciousness is of.": James, 1904a, p. 1151.

p. 26:   In this essay "sciousness" and "pure experience" ... combination.: In addition to replacing "sciousness," "pure experience" was also used by James in the more general sense of "directly lived experience."

p. 26:   "... while James claimed ignorance of Buddhism": James, 1902/1987, p. 466.

p. 26:   "*to know immediately ... or intuitively ... identical*": James, 1894, p. 1062.

p. 27:   "When Fa-ch'ang was dying ... and nothing else.": Watts, 1957, p. 201.

p. 27:   "no dualism of being represented ... in the experience": James, 1904a, p. 1151.

p. 27:   "*naïf* immediacy ... "retrospection.": *Ibid.*

p. 27:   "account of the 9th-century monk, Xiangyan.": See Cleary, p. 265.

p. 28:   "glanced at the planet Venus ... sky.": Kapleau, p. 31.

p. 28:   "one-thought-instant" (*ekaksana*) and "no-thought-instant" (*aksana*): Suzuki, 1956, p. 268.

p. 28: "staining, fringe, or halo of obscurely felt relation to masses of other imagery.": James, 1890, p. 452.

p. 28: "pure *onsense!*": James, 1897, p. 678, writing under the influence of nitrous oxide.

p. 29: "this most fundamental experience ... beyond differentiation.": Loy, p. 136.

p. 29: Buddhists distinguished ... "(without-bifurcated-thought construction).": Loy, pp. 42-43.

p. 29: "when 'self' and 'other' ... very essence of Tao.": Loy, p. 34.

p. 30: Zen's "suchness" or "this-as-it-is-ness": Suzuki, p. 16.

p. 30: "immediate experience in its passing" ... "reality intended thereby.": James, 1904a, p. 1151.

p. 30: "always 'truth'" prime reality: *Ibid.*

pp. 30-31: "How, if 'subject' and 'object' ... 'out of one's own head?'": *Ibid.*, p. 1154.

p. 31: "Mental knives may be sharp, but they won't cut real wood.": *Ibid.*, p. 1155.

p. 31: "'Matter,' as something *behind* physical phenomena," is merely a "postulate" of thought.: James, 1890, p. 291, emphasis added.

p. 32: "If a man has experienced the inexpressible ... to express it.": Though commonly cited, it may be apocryphal.

p. 34: The palpable presence of an absence ... described by Sartre in *Being and Nothingness*: Sartre, pp. 6-12.

p. 35: "To forget the self" ... "is to be actualized by myriad things.": Dogen, in Tanashi, p. 70.

p. 35: "If we could say in English 'it thinks' ... minimum of assumption.": James, 1890, p. 220.

p. 36: "If ... the thought be ... some element of what it knows?": *Ibid.*, p. 268.

p. 36: "not one of these assumptions is true.": *Ibid.*

p. 36: confusing a thought with what the thought "can be developed into.": *Ibid.*

p. 36: the "conscious constitution" of the thought is not one of plurality but of unity.: *Ibid.*

p. 36: an "entirely different subjective phenomenon" than the thought "the pack of cards" or "the table.": *Ibid.*

pp. 36-37: "*Whatever things are thought in relation ... a single psychosis, feeling, or state of mind.*": *Ibid.*

p. 37: cannot "be made lighter" by assuming that it happens "inside the mind.":

Ibid., pp. 343-344.

p. 37:   is to assume ... a "chaotic manifold" that needs to be "reduced to order.": *Ibid.*, p. 344.

p. 38:   "Although Kant's name for it ... short enough.": James, *Ibid.*, p. 342.

p. 38:   Kant's description of "the facts" was "mythological" ... "as ineffectual and windy an abortion as Philosophy can show.": *Ibid.*

p. 38:   brought together in an "internal machine-shop" in the mind: *Ibid.*

p. 38:   "Experiences come on an enormous scale ... we can not begin to understand.": James, 1905, pp. 1190-1191.

p. 39:   Mozart, in the act of composing ... "all at once," in a "single glance of the mind": Mozart, quoted in James, 1890, p. 247.

p. 39:   "a constant 'self' moving through successive experiences": Watts, 1957, p. 123.

p. 39:   "*Succession is the thing.*": Skrupskelis, p. 230.

p. 41:   "Why do they not copy ... a dead fire?": Huang Po, p. 61.

p. 42:   James likens such transitions ... "perchings.": James, 1890, p. 236.

p. 42:   "we ought to say a feeling of *and*, a feeling of *if* ... a feeling of *blue* and *cold*.": James, 1890, p. 238.

pp. 42-43: "[I]f the plain facts be admitted ... absolutely unique pulse of thought.": *Ibid.*, pp. 472-473.

p. 43:   "The thinking of the sequence of B upon A ... then brought forth B.": James, *Ibid.*, p. 592, emphasis added.

p. 43:   "... successive ideas are not yet ... the thought *of* succession.": James, *Ibid.*

p. 43:   Kant called "bare succession" ... "vanishing and recommencing of thoughts": Kant, p. 214.

pp. 43-44: "'combining' or 'synthesizing' two ideas [m and n] ... "pulse of thought knowing two facts.": James, 1890, p. 473.

p. 44:   "An elastic ball ... in all these states.": Kant, p. 342.

pp. 44-45: "it is a patent fact of consciousness that a transmission like this actually occurs": James, 1890, p. 322.

p. 45:   Capitalizing the word "thought" to mean "the present mental state": *Ibid.*, p. 321.

p. 45:   "Each pulse of cognitive consciousness ... later proprietor.": *Ibid.*, p.322.

p. 45:   "sequence of differents.": Shadworth Hodgson, quoted by James, *Ibid.*, p. 224.

p. 45:   "directly verifiable existent" — "the passing Thought itself.": James, 1890, pp. 328, 379.

p. 46:   "Many years ago, I was working ... and stay there.": Wolinsky, p. 41.

p. 46:   "a one thought-instant": Suzuki, 1997, p. 268.

p. 46:   "small enough pulses" ... mediated by the passing thoughts themselves.: James, 1909b, p. 760.

p. 46:   "minimal fact" of experience ... a 'passing' moment experienced as difference.: *Ibid.*

p. 46:   they do not go "indissolubly" into each other, "with no dark spot" between them: *Ibid.*, pp. 759, 760.

p. 46:   are separated by the very "darkness" "out of" which they come.: *Ibid.*, p. 759.

p. 46:   "apparition.": James used his mystical coach Blood's phrase "apparition of difference," without attribution, in his essay "The Continuity of Experience." He quotes it again, with attribution, in his homage to Blood, "A Pluralistic Mystic," the last essay James published. See James, 1910b, p. 1298.

pp. 46-47: "If you watch very carefully ... thought process.": Krishnamurti, p. 226.

p. 47:   "at the death of each moment there is a gap ... the arising of the next.": Ray, pp. 330, 333.

p. 47:   6,460,000 such moments in 24 hours ... one thought per 20 milliseconds.: Hameroff & Penrose, p. 20.

p. 47:   as has been argued recently for visual consciousness ... derivable from moments: discrete "static snapshots": Crick & Koch, p. 122.

p. 48:   Individual visual perceptual moments also have a speed limit ... hundred milliseconds.: Sacks, 2004a, p. 10.

p. 48:   "Any content of consciousness" ... "has a survival time of only three seconds.": Pöppel, p. 62.

p. 48:   "if a mental state ceased to vary, its duration would cease to flow.": Bergson, p. 4. James championed Bergson's insistence that reality was inherently a dynamic process.

pp. 48-49: "... snap-shots taken ... eludes conceptual explanation altogether.": James, 1909b, p. 736.

p. 49:   "life in its original coming": *Ibid.*

p. 49:   "We may find movies convincing ... apparently continuous flow.": Sacks, 2004a., p. 7 (Sacks particularly relied on the studies of Dale Purves.).

p. 49:   "bursts of neural energy": Floyd, p. 262.

p. 50:   (corresponding to the theta rhythm of monks in Zazen): See Austin, p. 89.

p. 50:   "the viewer could then begin to distinguish ... motion is created.": Floyd, p. 261.

p. 50:   "all motion in what passes for the physical universe has dropped dead still.": *Ibid.*, p. 263.

pp. 50-51: "I got up from my meditation bed ... not to be running.": Lu K'uan Yü, p. 77.

p. 51:   consciousness can be "brought to a halt, stopped dead, for substantial periods": Sacks, 2004a, p. 6.

p. 51:   "Once I was called to the ward ... just an inch of water in the bath.": *Ibid.*, p. 5.

p. 52:   "discrimination of successions ... we only noted one": James, 1890, p. 602.

p. 52:   "there is a curious increase ... get to the end of it.": *Ibid.*

p. 52:   "processes seem to fade rapidly ... subdivisibility of successions.": *Ibid.*

p. 52:   For some patients with Parkinson's ... "exceptionally fast.": Sacks, 2004b, p. 66.

p. 52:   For others the hands move slowly.: *Ibid.* Sacks gives a vivid account of two such contrasting patients.

p. 53:   time is a "patently artificial" "construction.": James, 1907, p. 564.

p. 53:   *"There is no internal self or soul ... independent soul idea.":* John, p. 396.

p. 53:   "non-regressive satori": Loy, p. 150. See, too, the visual aid representing this state that a Theravada monk sketched for Loy, pp. 144-145.

p. 54:   "some shading or other of relation" or "inward coloring": James, 1890, p. 238.

p. 55:   "*in* the stream of consciousness.": *Ibid.*, p. 286, emphasis added.

p. 56:   James himself suggests this possibility ... "eddies" in the stream of thought.: James, 1890, pp. 427-428.

p. 56:   "The ego is a kind of flip ... the same as anxiety.": Watts, 1962, p. 72.

p. 57:   "If anyone urge that I assign no *reason* ... meaning of the world.": *Ibid.*, p. 379. In an essay published in the last year of his life, James "suggested" that the total sense or meaning of the world was no so much generated as *uncovered*. See James, 1910a.

p. 57:   "If you say that experience depends ... itself the experiencer.": Shankara, p. 80.

p. 57:   *"If the passing thought be the directly ... need not look beyond.":* James, 1890, p. 379. James and Shankara converge on the primacy of non-dual over dual

Bricklin

experience. They diverge on the inferences that follow.

p. 58: "First of all, I am aware … an unfriendly part thereto.": James, 1890, p. 286.

p. 59: " … *active* element in all consciousness … to be received by it": *Ibid.*, p. 285.

p. 59: while James himself sought to affirm this active element through his defense of free will: James, 1890, pp. 1086-1193.

p. 59: the grounds of his defense were not based … but on what he wanted to believe.: See Bricklin.

p. 59: No one, James reluctantly declared … "*contributes* energy to the result.": James, 1890, p. 428.

p. 60: "to have no wants is divine.": Xenophon, p. 71.

p. 62: "The *mutual* inconsistencies and agreements … that all men might use.": James, 1890, pp. 286-287, emphasis added.

p. 63: His paradigm of free will … produced a "mutual" relationship between them.: *Ibid.*, p. 428.

p. 65: "the darkest in the whole series" … dead and gone.": James, 1890, p. 323. James credits his colleague Shadworth Hodgson with the terminology "darkest."

p. 65: the present "practically cognized" … between the past and the future.": E. R. Clay, quoted by James, 1890, p. 574.

p. 65: Such specious present … "two directions of time.": *Ibid.*, p. 574.

p. 65: "*must* exist, but that it *does* exist … our immediate experience.": *Ibid.*, p. 573.

p. 65: "presence is really the negation of time" … not "content.": Bradley, p. 43. Bradley's exact quote is: "It is not the time that can ever be present, but only the content."

p. 65: "has no breadth, for if it had … middle of the breadth": Blood, quoted by James, 1910b, p. 1298.

p. 66: "*duration-block*" present: James, 1890, p. 574.

p. 66: present's "just past" "rearward portion": *Ibid.* pp. 609-610.

p. 66: "One evening, when Eleanor and I were walking home … with a feather.": Watts, 1973, pp. 152-153.

p. 66: "The past is nowhere." The future, too.: Bohm, p. 232.

p. 68: "For a peaceful meditation … cool and refreshing.": Suzuki, 1959, p. 79

p. 68: "[Morphine] doesn't quiet the pain … depersonalizes the pain.": In Brown, p. 119.

p. 69: "… he never spoke in anger … he ever felt it.": Bucke, quoted by James,

84

1902, p. 83.

p. 69:   "the whole body is elevated ... he is a god walking the earth.": Allen, p. 194.

p. 69:   "the Christ likeness": See Kaplan, picture no. 17.

p. 69:   "the marvelous transformation" ... both in the iris and the white": Allen, p. 194.

p. 72:   "... reinforcements and obstructions which obtain ... spontaneity": James, 1890, pp. 286-287.

p. 72:   "Having ... abandoned favoring and opposing ... neither-painful-or-pleasant.": *Mahatanhasankhaya*, Sutta 38, in Bhikkus, p. 360.

p. 73:   every encounter "is subdued into sustenance.": Whitman, quoted by Allen, p. 194.

p. 73:   was extolled by James in a talk he gave to students: James, 1899.

p. 73:   "mystic ontological emotion ... contractile elements": James, 1902, p. 83.

p. 73:   "divert[s] our attention ... "disease and death.": *Ibid.*, pp. 87-88.

p. 73:   "Behold this compost ... yet behold!": Whitman, p. 294.

p. 74:   "[S]he took cognizance of things ... moment which came after.": Upham, T.C., quoted by James, 1902, p. 265.

p. 74:   James lamented that his own "constitution" ... mystical experiences.: James, 1902, p. 342.

III.

The independent reality of objects, said James, is an "indestructible common-sense assumption."[*] He should know. For despite his "central thesis" that "subjectivity and objectivity are affairs not of what an experience is aboriginally made of, but of its classification,"[†] he could not live outside that classification any more than a weekend meditator. To "traverse common-sense . . . in philosophy" was "no insuperable objection"[††] for him; but generating this *particular* objection to common-sense made him

> ". . . inwardly sick with the fever . . . . It is a sort of madness . . . when it is on you. The total result is to make me admire 'Common Sense' as having done by far the biggest stroke of genius ever made in philosophy when it reduced the chaos of crude experience to order by its luminous *Denkmittel* [means of thinking] of the stable 'thing,' and its dualism of

---

[*] Letter to Ferdinand Canning Scott Schiller, 20 March 1908.

[†] James, William (1905), "The Place of Affectional Facts in a World of Pure Experience," in *William James: Writings 1902-1910* (New York: Library of America, 1987), p. 1208.

[††] James, William (1890/1983), *The Principles of Psychology* (Cambridge, MA: Harvard University Press), p. 291.

thought and matter."*

James's admiration for dualistic common-sense stayed with him, despite his own biggest stroke of genius that "things and thoughts are not at all fundamentally heterogeneous."† Lingering dualism can be found, for example, in his 1904 essay, "A World of Pure Experience," and in letters he wrote years later.†† But when he came to summarize his philosophy of pure experience in 1905, before an international conference of his peers, common-sense dualism is annihilated. This summary, entitled "Notion of Consciousness," is James's concisest statement of the primacy of non-dual reality. It deserves a place beside *Zen Mind, Beginners Mind* as a luminous destroyer of what is, after all, only the common-sense of the West.

—J.B.

---

* Letter to Dickinson Sergeant Miller, 18 August 1903.

† See p. 110.

†† In a 1907 letter to the philosopher Augustus Strong he wrote: "It seems as if the whole world had conspired to insist that I shall not be a realist, in spite of anything I may say I am to the contrary." Previously he had written Strong that "the reality known exists independently of the knower's idea and as conceived, if the conception be a true one. I can see that some bad parturient phrases of my radical empiricism might lead to an opposite interpretation, but if so they must be expunged."

The Notion of Consciousness

by William James

Communication made (in French) at the
5th International Congress of Psychology
Rome, 30 April 1905
A new translation† by Jonathan Bricklin

I should like to convey to you some doubts which
have occurred to me on the subject of the notion of
consciousness that prevails in all our treatises on psychology.

Psychology is usually defined as the Science of
the facts of Consciousness, or the *phenomena* or, yet,
the *states* of Consciousness. Whether one admits that
it is connected to personal egos, or believes it to be
impersonal after the fashion of Kant's 'transcendental
ego,' the *Bewusstheit* [awareness] or the *Bewusstsein
überhaupt* [consciousness in general] of our German
contemporaries, this consciousness is always regard-

---

† Originally translated by Salvatore Saladino for a 1967 Random House An-
thology, and subsequently amended by Harvard University Press (unattrib-
uted). My motivation to re-translate was to adhere more closely to James's
precise thought, as well as to utilize English terms and phraseology found
elsewhere in his published work. All translators are indebted to those who
go before them, and many of Saladino's graceful constructions have been re-
tained. (According to the *DeltaView* program there are 964 changes between
our two versions.) I am also indebted to French writer Isabelle Deconinck,
who made corrections and suggestions throughout, and to Eugene Taylor.
— J.B.

ed as possessing its own essence, absolutely distinct from the essence of material things, which has the mysterious capacity* of representing and knowing. The material facts, taken in their materiality, are not *felt*, are not objects of *experience*, nor are they *related*. In order that they may assume the form of the system in which we feel ourselves to be living, it is necessary that material facts *appear*; and this fact of appearing, superadded to their bare existence, is called the consciousness which we have of them, or perhaps, according to the panpsychical hypothesis, which they have of themselves.

There you have it: this inveterate dualism which it seems impossible to dismiss from our view of the world. This world may well exist in itself, but we know nothing of this, because for us it is exclusively an object of experience; and the indispensable condition to this end is that it be related to witnesses, that it be known by a mental subject or subjects. Object and subject, *voilà*: the two legs without which it seems philosophy would not know how to take a step forward.

All the schools are in agreement on it — Scholastic, Cartesian, Kantian, Neo-Kantian — all admit to a fundamental dualism. The positivism or agnosticism of our day, which prides itself as coming

* *don*: gift, talent, aptitude or capacity. — J.B.

under the physical sciences, is readily given, it is true, the name of monism. But it is only a verbal monism. It posits an unknown reality, but tells us that this reality always presents itself under two 'aspects,' one side consciousness and one side matter; and these two sides remain as irreducible as the fundamental attributes, extension and thought, of the God of Spinoza. At bottom, contemporary monism is pure Spinozism.

Now, how to portray this consciousness whose existence we are all so disposed to admit? Impossible to define it, we are told, but we all have an immediate intuition of it: first of all, consciousness is conscious of itself. Ask the first person you meet, man or woman, psychologist or layman, and he will tell you that he *feels* himself thinking, enjoying, suffering, willing, just as he feels himself breathing. He perceives directly his mental life as a sort of inner stream, active, light, fluid, delicate, diaphanous, so to speak, and absolutely opposed to whatever is material. In short, subjective life seems to be not only a logically indispensable condition for there to be an objective world which *appears*, it is also an element of experience itself which we feel directly, in the same way that we feel our own body.

Ideas and Things: how then not to recognize their dualism? Feelings and Objects: how to doubt their absolute heterogeneity?

So-called scientific psychology admits this heterogeneity as the old spiritualist psychology admitted it. How not to admit it? Every science arbitrarily cuts out of the fabric of facts a field where it lodges itself, and the content of which it describes and studies. Psychology takes precisely for its domain the field of the facts of consciousness. It postulates them without criticizing them, it opposes them to material facts; and without criticizing, also, the notion of the latter, it attaches them to consciousness by the mysterious bond of *knowing*, of *apperception*, which, for it, is a third kind of fundamental and ultimate fact. By following this approach, contemporary psychology has enjoyed great triumphs. It has been able to make a sketch of the evolution of conscious life, by conceiving the latter as adapting itself more and more completely to the environing physical world. It has been able to establish a parallelism within the dualism, that of psychical facts and cerebral events. It has explained delusions, hallucinations, and, up to a certain point, mental illnesses. These are handsome achievements; but many problems yet remain. Above all, general philosophy, which has as its task the scrutiny of all postulates, finds paradoxes and obstacles precisely where science takes no notice; and only amateurs of popular science are never perplexed. The more we get to the bottom of things, the more enigmas we find; and, for my part, I confess that since I began to concern myself seriously with psychology, this old dualism of matter and thought, this heterogeneity posited as an absolute of two essences, has always for me presented difficulties. It is several of these difficulties that I would like now to address.

To begin with, there is one, which, I am sure, has struck you all. Let us take outer perception, the direct sensation which the walls of this room, for example, give us. Can one say here that the psychical and the physical are absolutely heterogeneous? On the contrary, they are so little heterogeneous that if we adopt the common-sense point of view; if we disregard all the explanatory inventions, of molecules and ether waves, for example, which at bottom are metaphysical entities; if, in a word, we take reality naively and as it is given to us, all at once, this sensible reality on which our vital interests depend, and from which all our actions proceed; well! this sensible reality and the sensation which we have of it are, at the moment the sensation occurs, absolutely identical, one with the other. The reality is the apperception itself. The words, 'the walls of this room,' mean nothing but the fresh and resounding whiteness which surrounds us, interrupted by these windows, bounded by these lines and these angles. The physical here has no other content than the psychical. Subject and object merge.

It is Berkeley who first honored this truth. *Esse*

est percipi. Our sensations are not small inner duplicates of things, they are the things themselves in so far as the things are present to us. And whatever we want to think of the absent, hidden, and, so to speak, private life of things, and whatever may be the hypothetical constructions that one makes of it; it remains true that the public life of things, this present actuality by which they confront us, from which all our theoretical constructions are derived, and to which they must all return and be linked under penalty of floating in the air and in the unreal; this actuality, I say, is homogeneous, and not only homogeneous, but numerically one, with a certain part of our inner life.

So much for outer perception. When we address ourself to imagination, to memory, or to faculties of abstract representation — although the facts here are much more complicated — I believe that the same essential homogeneity is revealed. In order to simplify the problem, let us first exclude at the outset all sensible reality. Let us take pure thought, such as it occurs in dreaming or reveries, or in remembrance of the past. Here, too, does not the stuff of experience do double work; do not the physical and the psychical merge? If I dream of a mountain of gold, doubtless it does not exist outside of the dream; but *in* the dream the mountain is of a perfectly physical nature or essence, it is *as* physical that it appears to me. If at this moment I allow myself to recollect my home in America and some details of my recent embarkation for Italy, the pure phenomenon, the fact thus produced, what is it? It is, one says, my thought with its content. But, again, this content, what is it? It bears the form of a part of the real world, a distant part, it is true, six thousand kilometers in space and six weeks in time; but linked to the room where we are by a crowd of things, objects and events, homogeneous on the one hand with the room and on the other hand with the object of my recollection.

This content is not given as being at first a tiny inner fact which I would subsequently project into the distance; it presents itself from the outset as the distant fact itself. And the act of thinking this content, the consciousness that I have of it, what are they? Are they at bottom anything other than retrospective ways of naming the content itself, at the time when one will have separated it from all these physical intermediaries, and linking it to a new group of associates which make it re-enter into my mental life — the emotions, for example, which it has awakened in me, the attention which I bring there, my ideas just now which sparked it as a recollection? It is only as it relates to these latter associates that the phenomenon comes to be classed as *thought*; so long as it remains related to the physical intermediaries, it remains an *objective* phenomenon.

It is true that we usually oppose our inner representations to objects, and that we consider them as little copies, as enfeebled tracings or duplicates of the latter. It is simply that a present object has a vivacity and clarity superior to those of the representation. It thus serves as a contrast to it; and, to use Taine's excellent term, it acts as a *reductive* of it. When the two themselves are present together, the object takes the foreground and the image 'recedes,' it becomes an 'absent' thing. But this present object, what is it in itself? Of what stuff is it made? Of the same stuff as the image. It is made of *sensations*; it is a thing perceived. Its *esse* is *percipi*, and it and the representation are generically homogeneous.

If at this moment I think of my hat which a while ago I left in the cloakroom, where is the dualism, the discontinuity, between the thought hat and the real hat? It is a true *absent hat* my mind is occupied with. I reckon with it practically as with a reality. If it were present on this table, the hat would determine a movement of my hand: I would pick it up. In the same way, this hat conceived, this hat as idea, will presently determine the direction of my steps. I will go get it. The idea I have of it will last up to the sensible presence of the hat, and blend there harmoniously.

I therefore conclude that — although there be a practical dualism — inasmuch as representations are distinguished from objects, stand in their stead, and lead us to them, there is no ground to attribute to them an essential difference of nature. Thought and actuality are made of only one and the same stuff, which is the stuff of experience in general.

The psychology of outer perception leads us to the same conclusion. When I perceive the object before me as a table of such and such a shape, at such and such distance, I am told that this fact is due to two factors: to a sensible matter that penetrates into me by means of my eyes and which provides the element of real exteriority, and to ideas which are awakened, go to meet this reality, classify and interpret it. But who can distinguish in the table concretely perceived between what is sensation and what is idea? The external and the internal, the extended and the inextended, fuse and make an indissoluble marriage. This brings to mind those circular panoramas, in which real objects — rocks, grass, broken carts, etc., which occupy the foreground — are so ingeniously linked with the canvas backdrop on which there is represented a battle-scene or a vast landscape, that one can no longer distinguish between what is an object and what is a painting. The seams and joints are imperceptible.

Could this occur if object and idea were absolutely dissimilar in nature?

I am convinced that considerations similar to those I have just expressed will have already given rise to some doubts, in you as well, on the subject of so-called dualism.

Still other reasons for doubting arise. There is a whole sphere of adjectives and attributes which are neither objective nor subjective in an exclusive manner, but which we employ sometimes in one manner and sometimes in another, as if we take pleasure in their ambiguity. I am speaking of qualities which we *appreciate*, so to speak, in things: their aesthetic, moral side, their value for us. Beauty, for example, where does it reside? Is it in the statue, in the sonata, or in our mind? My colleague at Harvard, George Santayana, has written a book on aesthetics, in which he calls beauty 'pleasure objectified'; and, in truth, it is precisely in this case that one could speak of projection outward. We say, indiscriminately, an agreeable warmth, or an agreeable feeling of warmth. The rarity and preciousness of a diamond appear to us to be its essential qualities. We speak of a dreadful storm, a hateful man, a mean action, and we think to be speaking objectively, although these terms express only relations to our own emotional sensibility. We even say a weary road, a sullen sky, a superb sunset. This whole animistic way of looking at things, which appears to have been mankind's earliest manner of thinking, may very well be explained (and Mr. Santayana, in another and very recent book, has in fact explained it thus) by the practice of attributing to the object *everything* that we feel in its presence. The division of subjective and objective is the fact of a very advanced reflection, which we still like to put off in many cases. When practical needs do not of necessity pull us away from it, it seems that we like to indulge in the vague.

The secondary qualities themselves — heat, sound, light — have, even today, but a vague attribution. For common-sense, for practical life, they are absolutely objective, physical. For the physicist, they are subjective. For him, only form, mass, and movement have an outer reality. For the idealistic philosopher, on the contrary, form and movement are just as subjective as light and heat, and only the unknown thing-in-itself, the 'noumenon,' enjoys a completely extra-mental reality.*

Our intimate sensations still retain this ambiguity. There are illusions of movement which prove that our first sensations of movement were generalized. It is the entire world which moved, with us. Now we distinguish our own movement from that of the ob-

---

* The French, '*réalité extramentale complete*,' literally means 'an extramental reality that is complete.' I do not believe that is what James intended here. —J.B.

jects which surround us, and among the objects we distinguish those which remain at rest. But there are states of dizziness in which even today we fall back into the initial indifferentiation.*

You all know, undoubtedly, of that theory that has wanted to make emotions the sum of visceral and muscular sensations. It has given rise to many controversies, and no one opinion has yet won unanimous approval. You know, as well, of the controversies about the nature of mental activity. Some maintain that it is a purely spiritual force which we are in a condition to apperceive immediately as such. Others claim that that which we call mental activity (effort, attention, for example,) is only the felt reflection of certain effects of which our organism is the seat: muscular tensions in the skull and in the throat, arrest or passage of breathing, rush of blood, etc.

However these controversies may be resolved, their very existence proves one thing quite clearly: it is very difficult, or even absolutely impossible, to know, solely by intimate inspection of certain phenomena, whether they are of a physical nature, occupying space, etc., or whether they are of a purely psychical and inner nature. We must always find reasons to support our opinion; we must look for the most probable classification of the phenomenon; and

---

* Though now archaic, 'indifference,' in James's time, meant 'lack of difference or distinction between two or more things.' —J.B.

in the end we may well find that all our usual classifications have derived their motives more from practical needs than from some faculty we possess of ap-
perceiving two ultimate and diverse essences which
together would comprise the scheme of things. Our
own individual body offers a practical, almost violent,
contrast to all the rest of the environing world. All
that happens inside this body is more intimate and
important to us than that which happens elsewhere.
It is identified with our ego; it is classed with it. Soul,
life, breath, who can really distinguish between these
exactly? Even our representations and our memories,
which act upon the physical world only by means of
our body, seem to belong to the latter. We treat them
as inner, we classify them with our emotional feelings. We must admit, in short, that the question of
the dualism of thought and matter is very far from
being finally resolved.

And thus ends the first part of my address. I have
wanted to impress upon you, Ladies and Gentlemen,
my doubts and the reality, as well as the importance,
of the problem.

As for me, after long years of hesitation, I have
ended by making my choice squarely. I believe that
consciousness, as it is commonly represented, either
as an entity, or as pure activity, but in any case as
fluid, unextended, diaphanous, devoid of all content
of its own, but directly self-knowing — spiritual, in

short —, I believe, I say, that this consciousness is a pure chimera, and that the sum of concrete realities which the word consciousness should cover deserves a quite different description, a description, moreover, that a philosophy attentive to facts and capable of a little analysis should be henceforth in a position to provide, or, rather, to begin to provide. And these words bring me to the second part of my address. It will be much shorter than the first part, because if I were to develop it on the same scale, it would be far too long. It is necessary, therefore, that I limit myself to only indispensable indications.

Let us assume that consciousness, *Bewusstheit*, conceived as essence, entity, activity, irreducible half of every experience, is eliminated, that the fundamental and, so to speak, ontological dualism is abolished, and that what we suppose to exist is only what has been called until now the *content*, the *Inhalt*, of consciousness; how is philosophy going to escape the sort of vague monism which will result therefrom? I shall try to convey to you several positive suggestions on this matter, although I fear that, for lack of necessary development, my ideas will not shed a very great light. As long as I indicate the beginning of a path, it will perhaps be sufficient.

At bottom, why do we cling so tenaciously to this idea of a consciousness superadded to the existence of the content of things? Why do we lay claim to it so strongly, that whoever would deny it would seem to us more a practical joker than a thinker? Is it not in order to preserve this undeniable fact that the content of experience has not only an existence of its own, as immanent and intrinsic, but that each part of this content bleeds, so to speak, into its neighbors, gives an account of itself to others, in some way gets out of itself in order to be known, and that thereby the entire field of experience is found to be transparent from part to part, or constituted as a space which would be filled with mirrors?

This bilaterality of the parts of experience — namely, on the one hand, that they *are*, with qualities of their own; and, on the other hand, that they are related to other parts and are *known* — the prevailing opinion affirms, and explains it by a fundamental dualism of constitution belonging to each bit of experience as such. In this sheet of paper there is not only, we say, the content, whiteness, thinness, etc., but there is this second fact of the consciousness of this whiteness and this thinness. This function of being 'reported,' of being part of the entire fabric of a more comprehensive experience, is raised to an ontological fact, and one lodges this fact in the very interior of the paper, coupling it with the paper's whiteness and with its thinness. This is not an extrinsic relation that one supposes, it is half of the phenomenon itself.

I believe that, in short, we view reality as being constituted in the same way as the 'colors' are made that we use in painting. First there are the coloring materials, which correspond to the content; and there is a menstruum, oil or size,* which holds them in suspension, and which corresponds to consciousness. This is a complete dualism, in which, by using certain procedures, one can separate each element from the other by means of subtraction. It is thus that we are assured that by making a great effort of introspective abstraction, we can catch our consciousness in the quick, as a pure spiritual activity, while neglecting almost completely the materials which it illuminates at a given moment.

Now I ask you if we could not as easily completely reverse this way of viewing it? Let us suppose, indeed, that prime reality is of a neutral nature, and

* See "Does 'Consciousness' Exist," p. 118.

let us call it by some name also ambiguous, such as *phenomenon, datum,* or *Vorfindung* [finding]. As for me, I readily speak of it in the plural, and I give it the name of *pure experiences.* This will be a monism, if you want; but a monism altogether rudimentary and absolutely opposed to the so-called bilateral monism of positivism, scientific or Spinozistic.

These pure experiences exist and succeed one another, they enter into infinitely varied relations with one another, relations which are themselves essential parts of the fabric of experiences. There is a 'Consciousness' of these relations in the same way that there is a 'Consciousness' of their terms. As a result, groups of experiences are observable and distinguishable, and one and the same experience, given the great variety of its relations, can play a role in several groups at the same time. It is thus that in a certain context of associates it would be classed as a physical phenomenon, while in another entourage it would figure as a fact of consciousness, almost as the same particle of ink can belong simultaneously to two lines, the one vertical, the other horizontal,

Let us suppose, indeed, that prime reality is of a neutral nature, and let us call it by some name also ambiguous, such as *phenomenon, datum* . . . . As for me, I readily speak of it in the plural, and I give it the name of *pure experiences.*

provided the particle is situated at their intersection.

Let us take, in order to fix our ideas, the experience which we have at this moment of the place where we are, of these walls, of this table, of these chairs, of this space. In this full experience — concrete and undivided, just as it is there, a datum — the objective physical world and the personal inner world of each of us meet and fuse as lines fuse at their intersection. As a physical thing, this room is related to all the rest of the building, a building which we here do not know and shall not know. It owes its existence to a whole history of financiers, architects, workmen. It weighs on the ground; it will last indefinitely in time; if fire were to break out, the chairs and the table that it contains would be quickly reduced to ashes.

As a personal experience, by contrast, as something 'reported,' known, conscious, this room has completely other ins and outs. Its antecedents are not workmen; they are our respective thoughts of just a moment ago. Soon it will figure only as a fleeting fact in our biographies, associated with pleasant memories. As a psychical phenomenon, it hasn't any weight, its furniture is not combustible. It exerts no physical force other than on our brains alone, and many of us deny even that influence; whereas the physical room is in a relation of physical influence with all the rest of the world.

And yet it is absolutely the same room in both

cases. As long as we do not engage in speculative physics, as long as we root ourselves in common-sense, it is the room seen and felt which is definitely the physical room. Of what are we speaking, then, if not of *that*, of that same part of the material nature which all our minds, at this same moment, embrace, which enters such as it is into the actual and intimate experience of each one of us, and which our memory will consider always as an integral part of our history? It is absolutely a same stuff which figures simultaneously, according to the context in which one considers it, as a material and physical fact, or as a fact of intimate consciousness.

I believe, therefore, that one cannot treat consciousness and matter as being of disparate essence. We obtain neither one nor the other by subtraction, by neglecting each time the other half of an experience of double composition. The experiences are, on the contrary, originally of a rather simple nature. They *become* conscious in their entirety, they *become* physical in their entirety; and it is *by way of addition* that this result is achieved. In so far as experiences are prolonged in time, enter into relations of physical influence — breaking, warming, illuminating, etc., each other — we make of them a group apart which we call

. . . one cannot treat conscioness and matter as being of disparate essence.

the physical world. On the other hand, in so far as they are fleeting, physically inert, with a succession which does not follow a determined order, but seems rather to obey emotional vagaries, we make of them another group which we call the psychical world. It is by its entering at present into a great number of these psychical groups that this room becomes now a conscious thing, a reported thing, a known thing. In becoming henceforth a part of our respective biographies, it will not be followed by that dull and monotonous repetition of itself in time which characterizes its physical existence. It will be followed, on the contrary, by other experiences which will be discontinuous with it, or which will have that very particular kind of continuity which we call memory. Tomorrow it will have its place in each of our pasts; but the various presents to which all these pasts will be linked tomorrow will be quite different from the present which this room will enjoy tomorrow as a physical entity.

The two kinds of groups are made up of experiences, but the relations of the experiences among themselves differ from one group to the other. It is, therefore, by addition of other phenomena that a given phenomenon becomes conscious or known, and not by a splitting in two of an interior essence. Knowledge of things *supervenes* upon them; it is not immanent in them. It is not a fact either of a transcendental ego or of a *Bewusstheit* or act of consciousness which would animate each one of them. *They know each other*, or rather, there are some that know the others; and the relation which we call knowledge is itself, in many cases, only a series of intermediary experiences perfectly susceptible of being described in concrete terms. It is not at all the transcendent mystery in which so many philosophers have delighted.

But this would lead us too far off. I cannot enter here into all the innermost recesses of the theory of knowledge, or of what you Italians here call gnosiology. I must be satisfied with these abridged remarks, or simple suggestions, which are, I fear, still quite obscure for want of necessary developments.

Allow me, then, to sum up my views — too summarily and in a dogmatic style — in the following six theses:

(1) Consciousness, as it is ordinarily understood, does not exist, any more than does Matter, to which Berkeley has given the coup de grâce;

(2) What does exist and constitutes the portion of truth that the word 'Consciousness' covers over, is the susceptibility that the parts of experience possess to be reported or known;

(3) This susceptibility is explained by the fact that

certain experiences can lead to others by means of distinctly characterized intermediary experiences, in such a fashion that some are found to play the role of things known, the others that of knowing subjects;

(4) One can perfectly define these two roles without departing from the fabric of experience itself, and without invoking anything transcendent;

(5) The attributes subject and object, represented and representative, thing and thought mean, then, a practical distinction that is of the utmost importance, but that is of a FUNCTIONAL order only, and not at all ontological as classical dualism imagines it;

(6) Finally, things and thoughts are not at all fundamentally heterogeneous, but are made of one and the same stuff, a stuff which one cannot define as such, but only experience, and which one can call, if one wishes, the stuff of experience in general.

Notes

p. 89: This communication is a summary, by necessity very condensed, of views that the author has set forth, in the course of the last months, in a series of articles published in the *Journal of Philosophy, Psychology and Scientific Methods,* edited by M. Woodbridge (New York, 1904 and 1905).

p. 98: My colleague at Harvard, George Santayana, has written a book.: *The Sense of Beauty,* pp. 44 ff.

p. 99: Mr. Santayana, in another and very recent book: *The Life of Reason* [Vol. I, *Reason in Common Sense*, p. 142].

IV.

According to Alfred North Whitehead, "Does 'Consciousness' Exist?," was for our era what Descartes's *Discourse on Method* was for his: "the inauguration of a new stage in philosophy."* Written in 1904, in the pre-dawn hours of quantum physics and relativity, "Does 'Consciousness' Exist?" "open[ed] an epoch by . . . [the] clear formulation of terms in which thought could profitably express itself." Of course it was by "denying exactly what Descartes asserts" — a dualism of consciousness and matter — that James set the stage for our era. Descartes began his investigation into prime reality with the "I" of consciousness. But what happens when consciousness itself is the starting point?

—J.B.

* Whitehead, Alfred North (1925), *Science and the Modern World* (New York:MacMillan), p. 205.

Does 'Consciousness' Exist?

by William James (1904)

'Thoughts' and 'things' are names for two sorts of object, which common-sense will always find contrasted and will always practically oppose to each other. Philosophy, reflecting on the contrast, has varied in the past in her explanations of it, and may be expected to vary in the future. At first, 'spirit and matter,' 'soul and body,' stood for a pair of equipollent substances quite on a par in weight and interest. But one day Kant undermined the soul and brought in the transcendental ego, and ever since then the bipolar relation has been very much off its balance. The transcendental ego seems nowadays in rationalist quarters to stand for everything, in empiricist quarters for almost nothing. In the hands of such writers as Schuppe, Rehmke, Natorp, Münsterberg — at any rate in his earlier writings, Schubert-Soldern and others, the spiritual principle attenuates itself to a thoroughly ghostly condition, being only a name for the fact that the 'content' of experience *is known*. It loses personal form and activity — these passing over to the content — and becomes a bare *Bewusstheit* [awareness] or *Bewusstsein überhaupt* [consciousness

'consciousness,' . . . evaporated to . . . pure diaphaneity, is on the point of disappearing altogether. It is the name of a nonentity, and has no right to a place among first principles.

in general], of which in its own right absolutely nothing can be said.

I believe that 'consciousness,' when once it has evaporated to this estate of pure diaphaneity, is on the point of disappearing altogether. It is the name of a nonentity, and has no right to a place among first principles. Those who still cling to it are clinging to a mere echo, the faint rumor left behind by the disappearing 'soul' upon the air of philosophy. During the past year, I have read a number of articles whose authors seemed just on the point of abandoning the notion of consciousness, and substituting for it that of an absolute experience not due to two factors. But they were not quite radical enough, not quite daring enough in their negations. For twenty years past I have mistrusted 'consciousness' as an entity; for seven or eight years past I have suggested its non-existence to my students, and tried to give them its pragmatic equivalent in realities of experience. It seems to me that the hour is ripe for it to be openly and universally discarded.

To deny plumply that 'consciousness' exists seems so absurd on the face of it — for undeniably 'thoughts' do exist — that I fear some readers will follow me no farther. Let me then immediately explain that I mean only to deny that the word stands for an entity, but to insist most emphatically that it does stand for a function. There is, I mean, no aboriginal stuff or quality of being, contrasted with that of which material objects are made, out of which our thoughts of them are made; but there is a function in experience which thoughts perform, and for the performance of which this quality of being is invoked. That function is *knowing*. 'Consciousness' is supposed necessary to explain the fact that things not only are, but get reported, are known. Whoever blots out the notion of consciousness from his list of first principles must still provide in some way for that function's being carried on.

I.

My thesis is that if we start with the supposition that there is only one primal stuff or material in the world, a stuff of which everything is composed, and if we call that stuff 'pure experience,' then knowing can easily be explained as a particular sort of relation towards one another into which portions of pure experience may enter. The relation itself is a part of pure experience; one of its 'terms' becomes the subject or bearer of the knowledge, the knower,* the other becomes the object known. This will need much explanation before it can be understood. The best way to get it understood is to contrast it with the alternative view; and for that we may take the recentest alternative, that in which the evaporation of the definite soul-substance has proceeded as far as it can go without being yet complete. If neo-Kantism has expelled earlier forms of dualism, we shall have expelled all forms if we are able to expel neo-Kantism in its turn.

For the thinkers I call neo-Kantian, the word consciousness today does no more than signalize the fact that experience is indefeasibly dualistic in structure. It means that not subject, not object, but object-plus-subject is the minimum that can actually be. The subject-object distinction meanwhile is entirely different from that between mind and matter, from that between body and soul. Souls were detachable, had separate destinies; things could happen to them. To consciousness as such nothing can happen, for, timeless itself, it is only a witness of happenings in time, in which it plays no part. It is, in a word, but the logical correlative of 'content' in an Experience of which the peculiarity is that *fact comes to light* in it, that *awareness of content* takes place. Consciousness

* In my '*Psychology*' I have tried to show that we need no knower other than the 'passing thought.'

as such is entirely impersonal — 'self' and its activities belong to the content. To say that I am self-conscious, or conscious of putting forth volition, means only that certain contents, for which 'self' and 'effort of will' are the names, are not without witness as they occur.

Thus, for these belated drinkers at the Kantian spring, we should have to admit consciousness as an 'epistemological' necessity, even if we had no direct evidence of its being there.

But in addition to this, we are supposed by almost every one to have an immediate consciousness of consciousness itself. When the world of outer fact ceases to be materially present, and we merely recall it in memory, or fancy it, the consciousness is believed to stand out and to be felt as a kind of impalpable inner flowing, which, once known in this sort of experience, may equally be detected in presentations of the outer world. "The moment we try to fix our attention upon consciousness and to see *what*, distinctly, it is," says a recent writer, "it seems to vanish. It seems as if we had before us a mere emptiness. When we try to introspect the sensation of blue, all we can see is the blue; the other element is as if it were diaphanous. Yet it can be distinguished, if we look attentively enough, and know that there is something to look for." "Consciousness" (*Bewusstheit*), says another philosopher, "is inexplicable and hardly describable, yet all conscious experiences have this in common that what we call their content has this peculiar reference to a center for which 'self' is the name, in virtue of which reference alone the content is subjectively given, or appears. . . . While in this way consciousness, or reference to a self, is the only thing which distinguishes a conscious content from any sort of being that might be there with no one conscious of it, yet this only ground of the distinction defies all closer explanations. The existence of consciousness, although it is the fundamental fact of psychology, can indeed be laid down as certain, can be brought out by analysis, but can neither be defined nor deduced from anything but itself."

'Can be brought out by analysis,' this author says. This supposes that the consciousness is one element, moment, factor — call it what you like — of an experience of essentially dualistic inner constitution, from which, if you abstract the content, the consciousness will remain revealed to its own eye. Experience, at this rate, would be much like a paint of which the world pictures were made. Paint has a dual constitution, involving, as it does, a menstruum* (oil, size or what not) and a mass of content in the form of pigment suspended therein. We can get the pure men-

* "Figuratively speaking, consciousness may be said to be the one universal solvent, or menstruum, in which the different concrete kinds of psychic acts and facts are contained, whether in concealed or in obvious form." G.T. Ladd: *Psychology, Descriptive and Explanatory*, 1894, p. 30.

struum by letting the pigment settle, and the pure pigment by pouring off the size or oil. We operate here by physical subtraction; and the usual view is, that by mental subtraction we can separate the two factors of experience in an analogous way — not isolating them entirely, but distinguishing them enough to know that they are two.

II.

Now my contention is exactly the reverse of this. *Experience, I believe, has no such inner duplicity; and the separation of it into consciousness and content comes, not by way of subtraction, but by way of addition* — the addition, to a given concrete piece of it, of other sets of experiences, in connection with which severally its use or function may be of two different kinds. The paint will also serve here as an illustration. In a pot in a paint-shop, along with other paints, it serves in its entirety as so much saleable matter. Spread on a canvas, with other paints around it, it represents, on the contrary, a feature in a picture and performs a spiritual function. Just so, I maintain, does a given undivided portion of experience, taken in one context of associates, play the part of a knower, of a state of mind, of 'consciousness'; while in a different context the same undivided bit of experience plays the part of a thing known, of an objective 'content.' In a word, in one group it figures as a thought, in another group as a thing. And, since it can figure in both groups simultaneously we have every right to speak of it as subjective and objective both at once. The dualism connoted by such double-barrelled terms as 'experience,' 'phenomenon,' 'datum,' *'Vorfindung'* [finding] — terms which, in philosophy at any rate, tend more and more to replace the single-barrelled terms of 'thought' and 'thing' — that dualism, I say, is still preserved in this account, but reinterpreted, so that, instead of being mysterious and elusive, it becomes verifiable and concrete. It is an affair of relations, it falls outside, not inside, the single experience considered, and can always be particularized and defined.

The entering wedge for this more concrete way of understanding the dualism was fashioned by Locke when he made the word 'idea' stand indifferently for thing and thought, and by Berkeley when he said that what common-sense means by realities is exactly what the philosopher means by ideas. Neither Locke nor Berkeley thought his truth out into perfect clearness, but it seems to me that the conception I am defending does little more than consistently carry out the 'pragmatic' method which they were the first to use.

If the reader will take his own experiences, he will see what I mean. Let him begin with a perceptual experience, the 'presentation,' so called, of a physical object, his actual field of vision, the room he sits in, with the book he is reading as its center; and let him for the present treat this complex object in the common-sense way as being 'really' what it seems to be, namely, a collection of physical things cut out from an environing world of other physical things with which these physical things have actual or potential relations. Now at the same time it is just *those self-same things* which his mind, as we say, perceives; and the whole philosophy of perception from Democritus's time downwards has been just one long wrangle over the paradox that what is evidently one reality should be in two places at once, both in outer space and in a person's mind. 'Representative' theories of perception avoid the logical paradox, but on the other hand they violate the reader's sense of life, which knows no intervening mental image but seems to see the room and the book immediately just as they physically exist.

The puzzle of how the one identical room can be in two places is at bottom just the puzzle of how one identical point can be on two lines. It can, if it be situated at their intersection; and similarly, if the 'pure experience' of the room were a place of intersection of two processes, which connected it with different groups of associates respectively, it could be counted twice over, as belonging to either group, and spoken of loosely as existing in two places, although it would remain all the time a numerically single thing.

Well, the experience is a member of diverse processes that can be followed away from it along entirely different lines. The one self-identical thing has so many relations to the rest of experience that you can take it in disparate systems of association, and treat it as belonging with opposite contexts. In one of these contexts it is your 'field of consciousness'; in another it is 'the room in which you sit,' and it enters both contexts in its wholeness, giving no pretext for being said to attach itself to consciousness by one of its parts or aspects, and to outer reality by another. What are the two processes, now, into which the room-experience simultaneously enters in this way?

One of them is the reader's personal biography, the other is the history of the house of which the room is part. The presentation, the experience, the *that* in short (for until we have decided *what* it is it must be a mere *that*) is the last term of a train of sensations, emotions, decisions, movements, classifications, expectations, etc., ending in the present, and the first term of a series of similar 'inner' operations extending into the future, on the reader's part. On the other hand, the very same *that* is the *terminus ad quem* of a lot of previous physical operations, carpentering, papering, furnishing, warming, etc., and the *terminus a quo* of a lot of future ones, in which it will be concerned when undergoing the destiny of a physical room. The physical and the mental operations form curiously incompatible groups. As a room, the experience has occupied that spot and had that environment for thirty years. As your field of consciousness it may never have existed until now. As a room, attention will go on to discover endless new details in it. As your mental state merely, few new ones will emerge under attention's eye. As a room, it will take an earthquake, or a gang of men, and in any case a certain amount of time, to destroy it. As your subjective state, the closing of your eyes, or any instantaneous play of your fancy will suffice. In the real world, fire will consume it. In your mind, you can let fire play over it without effect. As an outer object, you must pay so much a month to inhabit it. As an inner content, you may occupy it for any length of time rent-free. If, in short, you follow it in the mental direction, taking it along with events of personal biography solely, all sorts of things are true of it which are false, and false of it which are true if you treat it as a real thing experienced, follow it in the physical direction, and relate it to associates in the outer world.

III.

So far, all seems plain sailing, but my thesis will probably grow less plausible to the reader when I pass from percepts to concepts, or from the case of things presented to that of things remote. I believe, nevertheless, that here also the same law holds good. If we take conceptual manifolds, or memories, or fancies, they also are in their first intention mere bits of pure experience, and, as such, are single *thats* which act in one context as objects, and in another context figure as mental states. By taking them in their first intention, I mean ignoring their relation to possible perceptual experiences with which they may be connected, which they may lead to and terminate in, and which then they may be supposed to 'represent.' Taking them in this way first, we confine the problem to a world merely 'thought of' and not directly felt or seen. This world, just like the world of percepts, comes to us at first as a chaos of experiences, but lines of order soon get traced. We find that any bit of it which we may cut out as an example is connected with distinct groups of associates, just as our perceptual experiences are, that these associates link themselves with it by different relations,* and that one forms the inner history of a person, while the other acts as an impersonal 'objective' world, either spatial and temporal, or else merely logical or mathematical, or otherwise 'ideal.'

The first obstacle on the part of the reader to seeing that these non-perceptual experiences have

---

* Here as elsewhere the relations are of course *experienced* relations, members of the same originally chaotic manifold of non-perceptual experience of which the related terms themselves are parts.

objectivity as well as subjectivity will probably be due to the intrusion into his mind of *percepts,* that third group of associates with which the non-perceptual experiences have relations, and which, as a whole, they 'represent,' standing to them as thoughts to things. This important function of non-perceptual experiences complicates the question and confuses it; for, so used are we to treat percepts as the sole genuine realities that, unless we keep them out of the discussion, we tend altogether to overlook the objectivity that lies in non-perceptual experiences by themselves. We treat them, 'knowing' percepts as they do, as through and through subjective, and say that they are wholly constituted of the stuff called consciousness, using this term now for a kind of entity, after the fashion which I am seeking to refute.*

Abstracting, then, from percepts altogether, what I maintain is, that any single non-perceptual experience tends to get counted twice over, just as a perceptual experience does, figuring in one context as an object or field of objects, in another as a state of mind: and all this without the least internal self-diremption on its own part into consciousness and content. It is all consciousness in one taking; and, in the other, all content.

---

* Of the representative functions of non-perceptual experience as a whole, I will say a word in a subsequent article: it leads too far into the general theory of knowledge for much to be said about it in a short paper like this.

I find this objectivity of non-perceptual experiences, this complete parallelism in point of reality between the presently felt and the remotely thought, so well set forth in a page of Münsterberg's *Grundzuge*, that I will quote it as it stands.

"I may only think of my objects," says Professor Münsterberg; "yet, in my living thought they stand before me exactly as perceived objects would do, no matter how different the two ways of apprehending them may be in their genesis. The book here lying on the table before me, and the book in the next room of which I think and which I mean to get, are both in the same sense given realities for me, realities which I acknowledge and of which I take account. If you agree that the perceptual object is not an idea within me, but that percept and thing, as indistinguishably one, are really experienced *there, outside,* you ought not to believe that the merely thought-of object is hid away inside of the thinking subject. The object of which I think, and of whose existence I take cognizance without letting it now work upon my senses, occupies its definite place in the outer world as much as does the object which I directly see."

"What is true of the here and the there, is also true of the now and the then. I know of the thing which is present and perceived, but I know also of the thing which yesterday was but is no more, and which I only remember. Both can determine my present conduct, both are parts of the reality of which I keep account. It is true that of much of the past I am uncertain, just as I am uncertain of much of what is present if it be but dimly perceived. But the interval of time does not in principle alter my relation to the object, does not transform it from an object known into a mental state. . . . The things in the room here which I survey, and those in my distant home of which I think, the things of this minute and those of my long-vanished boyhood, influence and decide me alike, with a reality which my experience of them directly feels. They both make up my real world, they make it directly, they do not have first to be introduced to me and mediated by ideas which now and here arise within me. . . . This not-me character of my recollections and expectations does not imply that the external objects of which I am aware in those experiences should necessarily be there also for others. The objects of dreamers and hallucinated persons are wholly without general validity. But even were they centaurs and golden mountains, they still would be 'off there,' in fairy land, and not 'inside' of ourselves."

This certainly is the immediate, primary, naïf, or practical way of taking our thought-of world. Were there no perceptual world to serve as its 'reductive,' in Taine's sense, by being 'stronger' and more genuinely 'outer' (so that the whole merely thought-of world seems weak and inner in comparison), our world of thought would be the only world, and would enjoy complete reality in our belief. This actually happens in our dreams, and in our day-dreams so long as percepts do not interrupt them.

And yet, just as the seen room (to go back to our late example) is *also* a field of consciousness, so the conceived or recollected room is *also* a state of mind; and the doubling-up of the experience has in both cases similar grounds.

The room thought-of, namely, has many thought-of couplings with many thought-of things. Some of these couplings are inconstant, others are stable. In the reader's personal history the room occupies a single date — he saw it only once perhaps, a year ago. Of the house's history, on the other hand, it forms a permanent ingredient. Some couplings have the curious stubbornness, to borrow Royce's term, of fact; others show the fluidity of fancy — we let them come and go as we please. Grouped with the rest of its house, with the name of its town, of its owner, builder, value, decorative plan, the room maintains a definite foothold, to which, if we try to loosen it, it tends to return and to reassert itself with force. With these associates, in a word, it coheres, while to other houses, other towns, other owners, etc., it shows no tendency to cohere at all. The two collections, first of its cohesive, and, second, of its loose associates, inevitably come to be contrasted. We call the first collection the system of external realities, in the midst of which the room, as 'real,' exists; the other we call the stream of our internal thinking, in which, as a 'mental image,' it for a moment floats.* The room thus again gets counted twice over. It plays two different roles, being *Gedanke* and *Gedachtes*, the thought-of-an-object, and the object-thought-of, both in one; and all this without paradox or mystery, just as the same material thing may be both low and high, or small and great, or bad and good, because of its relations to opposite parts of an environing world.

As 'subjective' we say that the experience represents; as 'objective' it is represented. What represents and what is represented is here numerically the same; but we must remember that no dualism of being represented and representing resides in the experience *per se*. In its pure state, or when isolated, there is no self-splitting

> . . . no dualism of being represented and representing resides in the experience *per se*. In its pure state, or when isolated, there is no self-splitting of it into consciousness and what the consciousness is 'of.'

---

* For simplicity's sake I confine my exposition to 'external' reality. But there is also the system of ideal reality in which the room plays its part. Relations of comparison, of classification, serial order, value, also are stubborn, assign a definite place to the room, unlike the incoherence of its places in the mere rhapsody of our successive thoughts.

of it into consciousness and what the consciousness is 'of.' Its subjectivity and objectivity are functional attributes solely, realized only when the experience is 'taken,' *i.e.*, talked-of, twice, considered along with its two differing contexts respectively, by a new retrospective experience, of which that whole past complication now forms the fresh content.

The instant field of the present is at all times what I call the 'pure' experience. It is only virtually or potentially either object or subject as yet. For the time being, it is plain, unqualified actuality or existence, a simple *that*. In this *naïf* immediacy it is of course *valid*; it is *there*, we *act* upon it; and the doubling of it in retrospection into a state of mind and a reality intended thereby, is just one of the acts. The 'state of mind,' first treated explicitly as such in retrospection, will stand corrected or confirmed, and the retrospective experience in its turn will get a similar treatment; but the immediate experience in its passing is always 'truth,'* practical truth, *something to act on,* at its own movement. If the world were then and there to go out like a candle, it would remain truth absolute and objective, for it would be 'the last word,' would have no critic, and no one would ever oppose the thought in it to the reality intended.[†]

* Note the ambiguity of this term, which is taken sometimes objectively and sometimes subjectively.

[†] In the *Psychological Review* for July of this year [1904], Dr. R.B. Perry has

I think I may now claim to have made my thesis clear. Consciousness connotes a kind of external relation, and does not denote a special stuff or way of being. *The peculiarity of our experiences, that they not only are, but are known, which their 'conscious' quality is invoked to explain, is better explained by their relations — these relations themselves being experiences — to one another.*

IV.

Were I now to go on to treat of the knowing of perceptual by conceptual experiences, it would again prove to be an affair of external relations. One experience would be the knower, the other the reality known; and I could perfectly well define, without the notion of 'consciousness,' what the knowing actually and practically amounts to — leading-towards, namely, and terminating-in percepts, through a series of transitional experiences which the world supplies. But I will not treat of this, space being insufficient.* I will rather consider a few objections that are sure to

published a view of Consciousness which comes nearer to mine than any other with which I am acquainted. At present, Dr. Perry thinks, every field of experience is so much 'fact.' It becomes 'opinion' or 'thought' only in retrospection, when a fresh experience, thinking the same object, alters and corrects it. But the corrective experience becomes itself in turn corrected, and thus experience as a whole is a process in which what is objective originally forever turns subjective, turns into our apprehension of the object. I strongly recommend Dr. Perry's admirable article to my readers.

* I have given a partial account of the matter in *Mind,* vol. X, p. 27, 1885, and in the *Psychological Review,* vol. II, p. 105, 1895. See also C.A. Strong's article in the *Journal of Philosophy, Psychology and Scientific Methods,* Vol. I, p. 253, May 12, 1904. I hope myself very soon to recur to the matter in this Journal.

be urged against the entire theory as it stands.

V.

First of all, this will be asked: "If experience has not 'conscious' existence, if it be not partly made of 'consciousness,' of what then is it made? Matter we know, and thought we know, and conscious content we know, but neutral and simple 'pure experience' is something we know not at all. Say *what* it consists of — for it must consist of something — or be willing to give it up!"

To this challenge the reply is easy. Although for fluency's sake I myself spoke early in this article of a stuff of pure experience, I have now to say that there is no *general* stuff of which experience at large is made. There are as many stuffs as there are 'natures' in the things experienced. If you ask what any one bit of pure experience is made of, the answer is always the same: "It is made of *that*, of just what appears, of space, of intensity, of flatness, brownness, heaviness, or what not." Shadworth Hodgson's analysis here leaves nothing to be desired. Experience is only a collective name for all these sensible natures, and save for time and space (and, if you like, for 'being') there appears no universal element of which all things are made.

VI.

The next objection is more formidable, in fact it sounds quite crushing when one hears it first.

"If it be the self-same piece of pure experience, taken twice over, that serves now as thought and now as thing" — so the objection runs — "how comes it that its attributes should differ so fundamentally in the two takings. As thing, the experience is extended; as thought, it occupies no space or place. As thing, it is red, hard, heavy; but who ever heard of a red, hard or heavy thought? Yet even now you said that an experience is made of just what appears, and what appears is just such adjectives. How can the one experience in its thing-function be made of them, consist of them, carry them as its own attributes, while in its thought-function it disowns them and attributes them elsewhere. There is a self-contradiction here from which the radical dualism of thought and thing is the only truth that can save us. Only if the thought is one kind of being can the adjectives exist in it 'intentionally' (to use the scholastic term); only if the thing is another kind, can they exist in it constitutively and energetically. No simple subject can take the same adjectives and at one time be qualified by it, and at another time be merely 'of' it, as of something only meant or known."

The solution insisted on by this objector, like many other common-sense solutions, grows the less satisfactory the more one turns it in one's mind. To begin with, *are* thought and thing as heterogeneous as is commonly said? . . . what part comes in through the sense organs and what part comes 'out of one's own head'?

No one denies that they have some categories in common. Their relations to time are identical. Both, moreover, may have parts (for psychologists in general treat thoughts as having them); and both may be complex or simple. Both are of kinds, can be compared, added and subtracted and arranged in serial orders. All sorts of adjectives qualify our thoughts which appear incompatible with consciousness, being as such, a bare diaphaneity. For instance, they are natural and easy, or laborious. They are beautiful, happy, intense, interesting, wise, idiotic, focal, marginal, insipid, confused, vague, precise, rational, causal, general, particular, and many things besides. Moreover, the chapters on 'Perception' in the Psychology-books are full of facts that make for the essential homogeneity of thought with thing. How, if 'subject' and 'object' were separated 'by the whole diameter of being,' and had no attributes and common, could it be so hard to tell, in a presented and recognized material object, what part comes in through the sense-organs and what part comes 'out of one's own head'? Sensations and apperceptive ideas fuse here so intimately that you can no more tell where one begins and the other ends, than you can tell, in those cunning circular panoramas that have lately been exhibited, where the real foreground and the painted canvas join together.*

Descartes for the first time defined thought as the absolutely unextended, and later philosophers have accepted the description as correct. But what possible meaning has it to say that, when we think of a foot-rule or a square yard, extension is not attributable to our thought? Of every extended object the *adequate* mental picture must have all the extension of the object itself. The difference between objective and subjective extension is one of relation to a context solely. In the mind the various extents maintain no necessarily stubborn order relatively to each other, while in the physical world they bound each other stably, and, added together, make the great enveloping Unit which we believe in and call real Space. As 'outer,' they carry themselves adversely, so to speak, to one another, exclude one another and maintain their distances; while, as 'inner,' their order is loose, and they form a *durcheinander* [chaos, confusion, jumble] in which unity is lost. But to argue from this that inner

---

* Spencer's proof of his 'Transfigured Realism' (his doctrine that there is an absolutely non-mental reality) comes to mind as a splendid instance of the impossibility of establishing radical heterogeneity between thought and thing. All his painfully accumulated points of difference run gradually into their opposites, and are full of exceptions.

experience is absolutely inextensive seems to me little short of absurd. The two worlds differ, not by the presence or absence of extension, but by the relations of the extensions which in both worlds exist.

Does not this case of extension now put us on the track of truth in the case of other qualities? It does; and I am surprised that the facts should not have been noticed long ago. Why, for example, do we call a fire hot, and water wet, and yet refuse to say that our mental state, when it is 'of' these objects, is either wet or hot? 'Intentionally,' at any rate, and when the mental state is a vivid image, hotness and wetness are in it just as much as they are in the physical experience. The reason is this, that, as the general chaos of all our experiences gets sifted, we find that there are some fires that will always burn sticks and always warm our bodies, and that there are some waters that will always put out fires; while there are other fires and waters that will not act at all. The general group of experiences that *act*, that do not only possess their natures intrinsically, but wear them adjectively and energetically, turning them against one another, comes inevitably to be contrasted with the group whose members, having identically the same natures, fail to manifest them in the 'energetic' way. I make for myself now an experience of blazing fire; I place it near my body; but it does not warm me in the least. I lay a stick upon it, and the stick either burns or remains green, as I please. I call up water, and pour it on the fire, and absolutely no difference ensues. I account for all such facts by calling this whole train of experiences unreal, a mental train. Mental fire is what won't burn real sticks; mental water is what won't necessarily (though of course it may) put out even a mental fire. Mental knives may be sharp, but they won't cut real wood. Mental triangles are pointed, but their points won't wound. With 'real' objects, on the contrary, consequences always accrue; and thus the real experiences get sifted from the mental ones, the things from our thoughts of them, fanciful or true, and precipitated together as the stable part of the whole experience-chaos, under the name of the physical world. Of this our perceptual experiences are the nucleus, they being the originally *strong* experiences. We add a lot of conceptual experiences to them, making these strong also in imagination, and building out the remoter parts of the physical world by their means; and around this core of reality the world of laxly connected fancies and mere rhapsodical objects floats like a bank of clouds. In the clouds, all sorts of rules are violated which in the core are kept. Extensions there can be indefinitely located; motion there obeys no Newton's laws.

VII.

There is a peculiar class of experiences to which,

whether we take them as subjective or as objective, we *assign* their several natures as attributes, because in both contexts they affect their associates actively, though in neither quite as 'strongly' or as sharply as things affect one another by their physical energies. I refer here to *appreciations*, which form an ambiguous sphere of being, belonging with emotion on the one hand, and having objective 'value' on the other, yet seeming not quite inner nor quite outer, as if a diremption had begun but had not made itself complete.

Experiences of painful objects, for example, are usually also painful experiences; perceptions of loveliness, of ugliness, tend to pass muster as lovely or as ugly perceptions; intuitions of the morally lofty are lofty intuitions. Sometimes the adjective wanders as if uncertain where to fix itself. Shall we speak of seductive visions or of visions of seductive things? Of wicked desires or of desires for wickedness? Of healthy thoughts or of thoughts of healthy objects? Of good impulses, or of impulses towards the good? Of feelings of anger, or of angry feelings? Both in the mind and in the thing, these natures modify their context, exclude certain associates and determine others, have their mates and incompatibles. Yet not as stubbornly as in the case of physical qualities, for beauty and ugliness, love and hatred, pleasant and painful can, in certain complex experiences, coexist.

If one were to make an evolutionary construction of how a lot of originally chaotic pure experience
became gradually differentiated into an orderly inner
and outer world, the whole theory would turn upon
one's success in explaining how or why the quality
of an experience, once active, could become less so,
and, from being an energetic attribute in some cases,
elsewhere lapse into the status of an inert or merely
internal 'nature.' This would be the 'evolution' of the
psychical from the bosom of the physical, in which
the esthetic, moral and otherwise emotional experiences would represent a halfway stage.

VIII.

But a last cry of *non possumus* will probably go
up from many readers. "All very pretty as a piece of
ingenuity," they will say, "but our consciousness itself
intuitively contradicts you. We, for our part, *know*
that we are conscious. We *feel* our thought, flowing
as a life within us, in absolute contrast with the objects which it so unremittingly escorts. We can not
be faithless to this immediate intuition. The dualism
is a fundamental *datum*: Let no man join what God
has put asunder."

My reply to this is my last word, and I greatly
grieve that to many it will sound materialistic. I can
not help that, however, for I, too, have my intuitions
and I must obey them. Let the case be what it may

in others, I am as confident as I am of anything that, in myself, the stream of thinking (which I recognize emphatically as a phenomenon) is only a careless name for what, when scrutinized, reveals itself to consist chiefly of the stream of my breathing. The 'I think' which Kant said must be able to accompany all my objects, is the 'I breathe' which actually does accompany them. There are other internal facts besides breathing (intracephalic muscular adjustments, etc., of which I have said a word in my larger Psychology), and these increase the assets of 'consciousness,' so far as the latter is subject to immediate perception; but breath, which was ever the original of 'spirit,' breath moving outwards, between the glottis and the nostrils, is, I am persuaded, the essence out of which philosophers have constructed the entity known to them as consciousness. *That entity is fictitious, while thoughts in the concrete are fully real. But thoughts in the concrete are made of the same stuff as things are.*

I wish I might believe myself to have made that

plausible in this article. In another article I shall try to make the general notion of a world composed of pure experiences still more clear.

Notes

p. 114:   . . . I have read a number of articles . . . abandoning the notion of consciousness: Articles by Bawden, King, Alexander, and others. Dr. Perry is frankly over the border.

p. 116:   In my *'Psychology'* ... the 'passing thought.': *Principles of Psychology,* Vol. I, pp. 338 ff. pp. 117-118: "The moment we try to fix our attention ... look for.": G.E. Moore: *Mind,* Vol. XII, N.S., [1903], p. 450.

p. 118:   "Consciousness . . . can neither be defined nor deduced from anything but itself.": Paul Natorp: *Einleitungindie Psychologie,* 1888, pp. 14, 112.

pp. 126-127: "What is true of the here and the there, ... in fairy land, and not 'inside' of ourselves.": Münsterberg: *Grundzuge Psychologie,* Vol. I, p. 48.

p. 128:   Grouped with . . . to reassert itself with force.: Cf. A.L. Hodder: *The Adversaries of the Sceptic,* pp. 94-99.

V.

The "immediately present moment" was analyzed by James in the following excerpt, written just prior to "Does 'Consciousness' Exist?" but not published in his lifetime. — J.B.

A Rustle of Wind

by William James

from the posthumously published manuscript,
The Many and the One

As I pause in my writing I perceive the rustling of the leaves of a breeze-swept maple hard-by. That rustling has gone on for many minutes, yet I only just now notice it. It probably gave me a 'sensation,' but the sensation lapsed immediately, for my Self of subsequent moments ignored and dropped it. What shall we call it? Was it 'rustling,' or was it 'sense of rustling'? Was it a mysterious two headed entity, both in one? What was it? Obviously what we mean by objective 'rustling' is just that pure experience; and that pure experience is also what we mean by sense of rustling. If there were no other experience in the world than that, the question whether it were objective or merely conscious, or both in one, would never have arisen. The rustling would be the world, and if anyone asked us then of what kind of stuff the world consisted, we should say of just *that* stuff, of *rustle*, if you need an appellation. It surely never would occur to us to say that it was composed of two stuffs "separated by the whole diameter of being" yet applied face to face in closest apposition: of *Inhalt* [content] and *Bewusstheit* [awareness], namely or of space-filling physical sound, and of non-spatial hearing sensibility. These attributions, this diremption, point to ulterior complications. We call the rustling physical when we come to connect it with other features of the tree and with the wind; we call it mental when we connect it with our listening and with the stream of our thinking which it interrupts.

Now the immediately present moment in everyone's experience, however complex the content of it may be, has this same absolute character. It rustles, so to speak. The vastest 'field of consciousness,' when *there*, does not yet figure either as a field of consciousness or as a reality outside. It figures as just *that*. So far as we tend to act on that, it is real naively or practically. So far as we reflect on it and criticize and 'reduce' it, it appears to us to have subjective status merely, to be a simple 'state of mind' of our own, one of our errors, or delusions perhaps. If, instead of reducing it, our reflection tends to confirm it, it then passes for real, no longer in the primary *naif* sense, but in the sense that expressly denies its subjectivity. Our percepts reduce our concepts and, unreduced themselves, constitute our world of material reality. But if we were to wake from our waking as we wake from dreams, our new transmundane experiences would reduce our [now formerly] present percepts and remand them also to subjective *status*. The last experience is always valid, the 'state of mind' one talks from is always true at its own moment, and if the world then ended, it would be absolutely true, for it would meet with no reductive.

The ordinary ontological dualism thus falls to the ground. Physical and mental being, thought-stuff and thing-stuff, are not two different kinds of material, separately existent, or the one serving as a sort of vehicle, or as an inner lining, or as a centre of reference, for the other. There is no stuff but pure experience-stuff, and whether a given bit of this shall be treated as a physical reality or as conscious state depends entirely on the context in which it is taken. It is an affair of functional relations and resultant classification exclusively, to which the stuff in its immediate nature is indifferent. *Esse* and *percipi* are identical, said Berkeley. He only failed to add that this applied to experiences in their original purity. In their second intention, as talked *about* or as entering into relation with other experiences, experiences of any kind whatever may figure, now as mental, now as physical exclusively, or else as partly both, or even as possessing simultaneously and coextensively both physical and mental aspects.

— William James (1988), *Manuscript Essays and Notes* (Cambridge, Mass.: Harvard University Press), pp. 29-31.

VI.

In the last year of his life, James characterized philosophy as an "ugly study," that did not offer "Ultimate Reality" in a "sublime and simple form." Written to a student in China who wanted to study philosophy in America, it evoked James's own aspirations as a young man. Philosophy was a late career move. James had first studied to be an artist.

It is a dictum of art that "seeing is forgetting the name of the thing you are looking at." James came to see in much of Western philosophy a reverse process: "the treating of a name as excluding from the fact named what the name's definition fails positively to include." James called this fact-exclusion "vicious intellectualism," the complete substitution of static "secondary formations" for the actual lived experience they are based upon. Like bad art, it "de-realized" life.

Pure experience sciousness is a response to this de-realization. In "Does 'Consciousness' Exist?" the dual experience of subject and object is itself revealed to be de-realized sciousness. In the following essay and the excerpts that follow, the de-realization is the "bad abstractionism" that maintains such dual experience through life's "passing pulses." James

never developed his philosophy of pure experience
sciousness beyond brief passages and essays. To do so
would have made it ugly.

— J.B.

A World of Pure Experience

by William James (1904)*

It is difficult not to notice a curious unrest in the philosophic atmosphere of the time, a loosening of old landmarks, a softening of oppositions, a mutual borrowing from one another on the part of systems anciently closed, and an interest in new suggestions, however vague, as if the one thing sure were the inadequacy of the extant school-solutions. The dissatisfaction with these seems due for the most part to a feeling that they are too abstract and academic. Life is confused and superabundant, and what the younger generation appears to crave is more of the temperament of life in its philosophy, even though it were at some cost of logical vigor and of formal purity. Transcendental idealism is inclining to let the world wag incomprehensibly, in spite of its Absolute Subject and his unity of purpose. Berkeleyan idealism is abandoning the principle of parsimony and dabbling in panpsychic speculations. Empiricism flirts with teleology; and, strangest of all, natural realism, so long decently buried, raises its head above the turf, and

* revised

finds glad hands outstretched from the most unlikely quarters to help it to its feet again. We are all biased by our personal feelings, I know, and I am personally discontented with extant solutions; so I seem to read the signs of a great unsettlement, as if the upheaval of more real conceptions and more fruitful methods were imminent, as if a true landscape might result, less clipped, straightedged and artificial.

If philosophy be really on the eve of any considerable rearrangement, the time should be propitious for any one who has suggestions of his own to bring forward. For many years past my mind has been growing into a certain type of *Weltanschauung.* Rightly or wrongly, I have got to the point where I can hardly see things in any other pattern. I propose, therefore, to describe the pattern as clearly as I can consistently with great brevity, and to throw my description into the bubbling vat of publicity where, jostled by rivals and torn by critics, it will eventually either disappear from notice, or else, if better luck befall it, quietly subside to the profundities, and serve as a possible ferment of new growths or a nucleus of new crystallization.

I. Radical Empiricism

I give the name of 'radical empiricism' to my *Weltanschauung.* Empiricism is known as the opposite of rationalism. Rationalism tends to emphasize universals and to make wholes prior to parts in the order of logic as well as in that of being. Empiricism, on the contrary, lays the explanatory stress upon the part, the element, the individual, and treats the whole as a collection and the universal as an abstraction. My description of things, accordingly, starts with the parts and makes of the whole a being of the second order. It is essentially a mosaic philosophy, a philosophy of plural facts, like that of Hume and his descendants, who refer these facts neither to Substances in which they inhere nor to an Absolute Mind that creates them as its objects. But it differs from the Humian type of empiricism in one particular which makes me add the epithet radical.

To be radical, an empiricism must neither admit into its constructions any element that is not directly experienced, nor exclude from them any element that is directly experienced. For such a philosophy, *the relations that connect experiences must themselves be experienced relations, and any kind of relation experienced must be accounted as 'real' as any thing else in the system.* Elements may indeed be redistributed, the original placing of things getting corrected, but a real place must be found for every kind of thing experienced, whether term or relation, in the final philosophic arrangement.

Now, ordinary empiricism, in spite of the fact

that conjunctive and disjunctive relations present themselves as being fully co-ordinate parts of experience, has always shown a tendency to do away with the connections of things, and to insist most on the disjunctions. Berkeley's nominalism, Hume's statement that whatever things we distinguish are as 'loose and separate' as if they had 'no manner of connection,' James Mill's denial that similars have anything 'really' in common, the resolution of the causal tie into habitual sequence, John Mill's account of both physical things and selves as composed of discontinuous possibilities, and the general pulverization of all Experience by association and the mind-dust theory, are examples of what I mean.

The natural result of such a world-picture has been the efforts of rationalism to correct its incoherencies by the addition of trans-experiential agents of unification, substances, intellectual categories and powers, or Selves; whereas, if empiricism had only been radical and taken everything that comes without disfavor, conjunction as well as separation, each at its face value, the results would have called for no such artificial correction. *Radical empiricism,* as I understand it, *does full justice to conjunctive relations,* without, however, treating them as rationalism always tends to treat them, as being true in some supernal way, as if the unity of things and their variety belonged to different orders of truth and vitality altogether.

II. Conjunctive Relations

Relations are of different degrees of intimacy. Merely to be 'with' one another in a universe of discourse is the most external relation that terms can have, and seems to involve nothing whatever as to farther consequences. Simultaneity and time-interval come next, and then space-adjacency and distance. After them, similarity and difference, carrying the possibility of many inferences. Then relations of activity, tying terms into series involving change, tendency, resistance, and the causal order generally. Finally, the relation experienced between terms that form states of mind, and are immediately conscious of continuing each other. The organization of the Self as a system of memories, purposes, strivings, fulfilments or disappointments, is incidental to this most intimate of all relations, the terms of which seem in many cases actually to compenetrate and suffuse each other's being.

Philosophy has always turned on grammatical particles. With, near, next, like, from, towards, against, because, for, through, my — these words designate types of conjunctive relation arranged in a roughly ascending order of intimacy and inclusiveness. *A priori*, we can imagine a universe of withness but no nextness; or one of nextness but no likeness, or of likeness with no activity, or of activity with no purpose, or of purpose with no ego. These would be universes, each with its own grade of unity. The universe of human experience is, by one or another of its parts, of each and all these grades. Whether or not it possibly enjoys some still more absolute grade of union does not appear upon the surface.

Taken as it does appear, our universe is to a large extent chaotic. No one single type of connection runs through all the experiences that compose it. If we take space-relations, they fail to connect minds into any regular system. Causes and purposes obtain only among special series of facts. The self relation seems extremely limited and does not link two different selves together. *Prima facie*, if you should liken the universe of absolute idealism to an aquarium, a crystal globe in which goldfish are swimming, you would have to compare the empiricist universe to something more like one of those dried human heads with which the Dyaks of Borneo deck their lodges. The skull forms a solid nucleus; but innumerable feathers, leaves, strings, beads, and loose appendices of every description float and dangle from it, and, save that they terminate in it, seem to have nothing to do with one another. Even so my experiences and yours float and dangle, terminating, it is true, in a nucleus of common perception, but for the most part out of sight and irrelevant and unimaginable to one another. This imperfect intimacy, this bare relation of *withness* between some parts of the sum total of experience and other parts, is the fact that ordinary empiricism over-emphasizes against rationalism, the latter always tending to ignore it unduly. Radical empiricism, on the contrary, is fair to both the unity and the disconnection. It finds no reason for treating either as illusory. It allots to each its definite sphere of description, and agrees that there appear to be actual forces at work which tend, as time goes on, to make the unity greater.

The conjunctive relation that has given most trouble to philosophy is the *co-conscious transition,* so to call it, by which one experience passes into another when both belong to the same self. About the facts there is no question. My experiences and your experiences are 'with' each other in various external ways, but mine pass into mine, and yours pass into yours in a way in which yours and mine never pass into one another. Within each of our personal histories, subject, object, interest and purpose *are continuous or may be continuous.** Personal histories are processes of change in time, and *the change itself is one of the things immediately experienced.* 'Change' in this case means continuous as opposed to discontinuous transition. But continuous transition is one sort of a conjunctive

* The psychology books have of late described the facts here with approximate adequacy. I may refer to the chapters on 'The Stream of Thought' and on the Self in my own *Principles of Psychology*, as well as to S.H.Hodgson's *Metaphysics of Experience*, Vol. I, Ch. VII and VIII.

relation; and to be a radical empiricist means to hold fast to this conjunctive relation of all others, for this is the strategic point, the position through which, if a hole be made, all the corruptions of dialectics and all the metaphysical fictions pour into our philosophy. The holding fast to this relation means taking it at its face value, neither less nor more; and to take it at its face value means first of all to take it just as we feel it, and not to confuse ourselves with abstract talk *about* it, involving words that drive us to invent secondary conceptions in order to neutralize their suggestions and to make our actual experience again seem rationally possible.

What I do feel simply when a later moment of my experience succeeds an earlier one is that though they are two moments, the transition from the one to the other is *continuous*. Continuity here is a definite sort of experience; just as definite as is the *discontinuity-experience* which I find it impossible to avoid when I seek to make the transition from an experience of my own to one of yours. In this latter case I have to get on and off again, to pass from a thing lived to another thing only conceived, and the break is positively experienced and noted. Though the functions exerted by my experience and by yours may be the same (*e.g.*, the same objects known and the same purposes followed), yet the sameness has in this case to be ascertained expressly (and often with dif-

ficulty and uncertainty) after the break has been felt;
whereas in passing from one of my own moments to
another the sameness of object and interest is unbro-
ken, and both the earlier and the later experience are
of things directly lived.

There is no other *nature*, no other whatness than
this absence of break and this sense of continuity in
that most intimate of all conjunctive relations, the
passing of one experience into another when they belong to the same self. And this whatness is real empirical 'content,' just as the whatness of separation and
discontinuity is real content in the contrasted case.
Practically to experience one's personal continuum in
this living way is to know the originals of the ideas
of continuity and sameness, to know what the words
stand for concretely, to own all that they can ever
mean. But all experiences have their conditions; and
over-subtle intellects, thinking about the facts here,
and asking how they are possible, have ended by substituting a lot of static objects of conception for the
direct perceptual experiences. "Sameness," they have
said, "must be a stark numerical identity; it can't run
on from next to next. Continuity can't mean mere
absence of gap; for if you say two things are in immediate contact, *at* the contact how can they be two?
If, on the other hand, you put a relation of transition
between them, that itself is a third thing, and needs
to be related or hitched to its terms. An infinite series

is involved," and so on. The result is that from difficulty to difficulty, the plain conjunctive experience
has been discredited by both schools, the empiricists
leaving things permanently disjoined, and the rationalists remedying the looseness by their Absolutes
or Substances, or whatever other fictitious agencies
of union they may have employed. From all which
artificiality we can be saved by a couple of simple
reflections: first, that conjunctions and separations
are, at all events, co-ordinate phenomena which, if
we take experiences at their face value, must be accounted equally real; and second, that if we insist
on treating things as really separate when they are
given as continuously joined, invoking, when union
is required, transcendental principles to overcome
the separateness we have assumed, then we ought to
stand ready to perform the converse act. We ought
to invoke higher principles of *dis*union, also, to make
our merely experienced *dis*junctions more truly real.
Failing thus, we ought to let the originally given
continuities stand on their own bottom. We have no
right to be lopsided or to blow capriciously hot and
cold.

III. The Cognitive Relation

The first great pitfall from which such a radical standing by experience will save us is an artifi-

cial conception of the *relations between knower and known*. Throughout the history of philosophy the subject and its object have been treated as absolutely discontinuous entities; and thereupon the presence of the latter to the former, or the 'apprehension' by the former of the latter, has assumed a paradoxical character which all sorts of theories had to be invented to overcome. Representative theories put a mental 'representation,' 'image,' or 'content' into the gap, as a sort of intermediary. Common-sense theories left the gap untouched, declaring our mind able to clear it by a self-transcending leap. Transcendentalist theories left it impossible to traverse by finite knowers, and brought an Absolute in to perform the bridging act. All the while, in the very bosom of the finite experience, every conjunction required to make the relation intelligible is given in full. Either the knower and the known are:*

(1) the self-same piece of experience taken twice over in different contexts; or they are

(2) two pieces of *actual* experience belonging to the same subject, with definite tracts of conjunctive

---

* For brevity's sake I altogether omit mention of the type constituted by knowledge of the truth of general propositions. This type has been thoroughly and, so far as I can see, satisfactorily, elucidated in Dewey's *Studies in Logical Theory*. Such propositions are reducible to the S-is-P form; and the 'terminus' that verifies and fulfils is the SP in combination. Of course percepts may be involved in the mediating experiences, or in the 'satisfactoriness' of the P in its new position.

transitional experience between them; or

(3) the known is a *possible* experience either of that subject or another, to which the said conjunctive transitions *would* lead, if sufficiently prolonged.

To discuss all the ways in which one experience may function as the knower of another, would be incompatible with the limits of this essay.* I have just treated of type 1, the kind of knowledge called perception [in "Does 'Consciousness' Exist?"]. This is the type of case in which the mind enjoys direct 'acquaintance' with a present object. In the other types the mind has 'knowledge-about' an object not immediately there. Of type 2, the simplest sort of conceptual knowledge, I have given some account in two articles.* Type 3 can always formally and hypothetically be reduced to type 2, so that a brief description of that type will put the present reader sufficiently at my point of view, and make him see what the actual meanings of the mysterious cognitive relation may be.

Suppose me to be sitting here in my library at Cambridge, at ten minutes' walk from 'Memorial Hall,' and to be thinking truly of the latter object.

* These articles ["On the Function of Cognition" (1885) and "The Knowing of Things Together" (1895)] and their doctrine, unnoticed apparently by any one else, have lately gained favorable comment from Professor Strong. Dr. Dickinson S. Miller has independently thought out the same results, which Strong accordingly dubs the James-Miller theory of cognition.

My mind may have before it only the name, or it may have a clear image, or it may have a very dim image of the hall, but such intrinsic differences in the image make no difference in its cognitive function. Certain extrinsic phenomena, special experiences of conjunction, are what impart to the image, be it what it may, its knowing office.

For instance, if you ask me what hall I mean by my image, and I can tell you nothing; or if I fail to point or lead you towards the Harvard Delta; or if, being led by you, I am uncertain whether the Hall I see be what I had in mind or not; you would rightly deny that I had 'meant' that particular hall at all, even though my mental image might to some degree have resembled it. The resemblance would count in that case as coincidental merely, for all sorts of things of a kind resemble one another in this world without being held for that reason to take cognizance of one another.

On the other hand, if I can lead you to the hall, and tell you of its history and present uses; if in its presence I feel my idea, however imperfect it may have been, to have led hither and to be now terminated; if the associates of the image and of the felt hall run parallel, so that each term of the one context corresponds serially, as I walk, with an answering term of the others; why then my soul was prophetic, and my idea must be, and by common consent would be, called cognizant of reality. That percept was what I *meant,* for into it my idea has passed by conjunctive experiences of sameness and fulfilled intention. Nowhere is there jar, but every later moment matches and corroborates an earlier one.

In this matching and corroborating, taken in no transcendental sense, but denoting definitely felt transitions, lies all that the knowing of a percept by an idea can possibly contain or signify. Wherever such transitions are felt, the first experience *knows* that last one. Where they do not, or where even as possibles, they can not, intervene, there can be no pretence of knowing. In this latter case the extremes will be connected, if connected at all, by inferior relations — bare likeness or succession, or by 'withness' alone. Knowledge thus lives inside the tissue of experience. It is *made;* and made by relations that unroll themselves in time. Whenever certain intermediaries are given, such that, as they develop towards their terminus, there is experience from point to point of one direction followed, and finally of one process fulfilled, the result is that their starting-point thereby becomes a knower and their terminus an object meant or known. That is all that knowing (in the simple case considered) can be known-as, that is the whole of its nature, put into experiential terms. Whenever such is the sequence of our experiences we may freely say that we had the terminal object 'in

mind' from the outset, even although *at* the outset
nothing was there in us but a flat piece of substantive
experience like any other, with no self-transcendency
about it, and no mystery save the mystery of coming into existence and of being gradually followed by
other pieces of substantive experience, with conjunc-
tively transitional experiences between. That is what
we *mean* here by the object's being 'in mind.' Of any
deeper more real way of being in mind we have no
positive conception, and we have no right to discredit
our actual experience by talking of such a way at all.

I know that many a reader will rebel at this.
"Mere intermediaries," he will say, "even though they
be feelings of continuously growing fulfilment, only
separate the knower from the known, whereas what
we have in knowledge is a kind of immediate touch
of the one by the other, an 'apprehension' in the ety-
mological sense of the word, a leaping of the chasm
as by lightning, an act by which two terms are smit-
ten into one, over the head of their distinctness. All
these dead intermediaries of yours are out of each
other, and outside of their termini still."

But do not such dialectic difficulties remind us
of the dog dropping his bone and snapping at its image in the water? If we knew anymore real kind of
union *aliunde* [from another source], we might be
entitled to brand all our empirical unions as a sham.
But unions by continuous transition are the only

ones we know of, whether in this matter of a knowledge-about that terminates in an acquaintance,
whether in personal identity, in logical predication
through the copula 'is,' or elsewhere. If anywhere
there were more absolute unions realized, they could
only reveal themselves to us by just such conjunctive
results. These are what the unions are *worth*, these
are all that *we can ever practically mean* by union, by
continuity. Is it not time to repeat what Lotze said
of substances, that to *act like one* is to *be* one? Should
we not say here that to be experienced as continuous is to be really continuous, in a world where experience and reality come to the same thing? In a
picture gallery a painted hook will serve to hang a
painted chain by, a painted cable will hold a painted
ship. In a world where both the terms and their distinctions are affairs of experience, conjunctions that
are experienced must be at least as real as anything
else. They will be 'absolutely' real conjunctions, if we
have no transphenomenal Absolute ready, to dereal-
ize the whole experienced world by, at a stroke. If,
on the other hand, we had such an Absolute, not one
of our opponents' theories of knowledge could remain standing any better than ours could; for the
distinctions as well as the conjunctions of experience
would impartially fall its prey. The whole question
of how 'one' thing can know 'another' would cease to
be a real one at all in a world where otherness itself

was an illusion.*

So much for the essentials of the cognitive relation, where the knowledge is conceptual in type,
or forms knowledge 'about' an object. It consists in
intermediary experiences (possible, if not actual) of
continuously developing progress, and, finally, of fulfilment, when the sensible percept, which is the object, is reached. The percept here not only *verifies* the
concept, proves its function of knowing that percept
to be true, but the percept's existence as the terminus
of the chain of intermediaries *creates* the function.
Whatever terminates that chain was, because it now
proves itself to be, what the concept 'had in mind.'

The towering importance of this kind of knowing for human life lies in the fact that an experience
that knows another can figure as its *representative,*
not in any quasi-miraculous 'epistemological' sense,
but in the definite practical sense of being its *substitute* in various operations, yet leading to the same result. By experimenting on our conceptual experiences
or ideas of reality, we may save ourselves the trouble
of experimenting on the real experience which they
severally mean. The ideas form related systems, corresponding point for point to the systems which the
realities form; and by letting an ideal term call up its

---

* Mr. Bradley, not professing to know his absolute *aliunde,* nevertheless de-
realizes Experience by alleging it to be everywhere infected with self-contradiction. His arguments seem almost purely verbal, but this is no place for
arguing that point out.

associates systematically, we may be led to a terminus which the corresponding real term would have led to in case we had operated on the real world. And this brings us to the general question of substitution.

IV. Substitution

In Taine's brilliant book on 'Intelligence,' substitution was for the first time named as a cardinal logical function, though of course the facts had always been familiar enough. What, exactly, in a system of experiences, does the 'substitution' of one of them for another mean?

According to radical empiricism, experience as a whole wears the form of a process in time, whereby innumerable particular terms lapse and are superseded by others that follow upon them by transitions which, whether disjunctive or conjunctive in content, are themselves experiences, and must in general be accounted at least as real as the terms which

. . . experience as a whole wears the form of a process in time, whereby innumerable particular terms lapse and are superseded by others that follow upon them by transitions which, whether disjunctive or conjunctive in content, are themselves experiences, and must in general be accounted at least as real as the terms which they relate.

they relate. What the nature of the event called 'superseding' signifies, depends altogether on the kind of transition that obtains. Some experiences simply abolish their predecessors without continuing them in any way. Others follow them more livingly, are felt to increase or to enlarge their meaning, to carry out their purpose, or to bring us nearer to their goal. They 'represent' them, and may fufil their function better than they fulfilled it themselves. But to 'fulfil a function' in a world of pure experience can be conceived and defined in only one possible way. In such a world transitions and arrivals (or terminations) are the only events that happen, though they happen by so many sorts of path. The only function that one experience can perform is to lead into another experience; and the only fulfilment we can speak of is the reaching of a certain experienced end. When one experience leads to (or can lead to) the same end as another, they agree in function. But the whole system of experiences as they are immediately given presents itself as a quasi-chaos through which one can pass out of an initial term in many directions and yet end in the same terminus, moving from next to next by a great many alternative paths.

Either one of these paths might be a functional substitute for another, and to follow one rather than another might on occasion be an advantageous thing to do. As a matter of fact, and in a general way, the

Wonderful are the new cuts and the short-circuits which the thought-paths make. Most thought-paths, it is true, are substitutes for nothing actual; they end outside the real world altogether, in wayward fancies, utopias, fictions or mistakes. But where they do re-enter reality and terminate therein, we substitute them always; and with these substitutes we pass the greater number of our hours.

This is why I called our experiences, taken all together, a quasi-chaos.

paths that run through conceptual experiences, that is, through 'thoughts' or 'ideas' that 'know' the things in which they terminate, are highly advantageous paths to follow. Not only do they yield inconceivably rapid transitions; but, owing to the 'universal' character* which they frequently possess, and to their capacity for association with one another in great systems, they outstrip the tardy consecutions of the things themselves, and sweep us on towards our ultimate termini in a far more labor-saving way than the following of trains of sensible perception ever could. Wonderful are the new cuts and the short-circuits which the thought-paths make. Most thought-paths, it is true, are substitutes for nothing actual; they end outside the real world

---

* Of which all that need be said in this essay is that it also can be conceived as functional, and defined in terms of transitions, or of the possibility of such.

altogether, in wayward fancies, utopias, fictions or mistakes. But where they do re-enter reality and terminate therein, we substitute them always; and with these substitutes we pass the greater number of our hours.

This is why I called our experiences, taken all together, a quasi-chaos. There is vastly more discontinuity in the sum total of experiences than we commonly suppose. The nucleus of every man's experience, the sense of his own body, is, it is true, a continuous perception; and equally continuous is his perception (though it may be very inattentive) of a material environment of that body, changing by gradual transition when the body moves. But the rest of the physical world is at all times absent from each of us, a conceptual object merely, into the perceptual realities of which our life inserts itself at points discrete and relatively rare. Round the nucleus, partly continuous and partly discrete, of what we call the physical world of actual perception, innumerable hosts of thinkers, pursuing their several lines of physically true cogitation, trace paths that intersect one another only at discontinuous perceptual points, and the rest of the time are quite incongruent; and around the whole of the nucleus of relative 'reality,' as around the Dyak's head of my late metaphor, there floats the vast *nimbus* of experiences that are wholly subjective, that are non-substitutional, that find not even an eventual ending for themselves in the perceptual world — the mere day-dreams and joys and sufferings and wishes of the individual minds. These exist *with* one another, indeed, and with the objective nucleus, but out of them it is probable that to all eternity no interrelated system of any kind will ever be made.

This notion of the purely substitutional or conceptual physical world brings us to the most critical of all steps in the development of a philosophy of pure experience. The paradox of self-transcendency in knowledge comes back upon us here, but I think that our notions of pure experience and of substitution, and our radically empirical view of conjunctive transitions, are *Denkmittel* [means of thinking] that will carry us safely through the pass.

V. What Objective Reference Is

Whosoever feels his experience as something substitutional, even while he has it, may be said to have an experience that reaches beyond itself. From inside of its own entity it postulates reality existing elsewhere. For the transcendentalist, who holds knowing to consist in a *salto mortale* [mortal leap] across an 'epistemological chasm,' such an idea presents no difficulty; but it seems at first sight as if it might be inconsistent with an empiricism like our own. Have we not explained conceptual knowledge to be wholly constituted by things that fall outside of the knowing experience itself — by intermediary experiences and by a terminus that fulfils? Can the knowledge be there before these elements that constitute its being have come? And, if knowledge be not there, how can objective reference occur?

The key to this difficulty lies in the distinction between knowing as verified and completed, and the same knowing as in transit and on its way. To recur to the Memorial Hall example lately used, it is only when our idea of the Hall has actually terminated in the percept that we know 'for certain' that from the beginning it was truly cognitive of *that*. Until established by the end of the process, its quality of knowing that, or indeed of knowing anything, could still be doubted; and yet the knowing really *was* there, as the result now shows. We were virtual knowers of the Hall long before we were nailed down and certified to have been its actual knowers, by the percept's retroactive validating power. Just so we are 'mortal' all the time, by reason of the virtuality of the inevitable event which will make us so when it shall have come.

Now the immensely greater part of all our knowing never gets beyond this virtual stage. It never is completed or nailed down. I speak not merely of our ideas of imperceptibles like ether-waves or dissociated 'ions,' or of 'ejects' like the contents of our neighbors'

We live, as it were, upon the front edge of an advancing wave-crest, and our sense of a determinate direction in falling forward is all we cover of the future of our path. It is as if a differential quotient should be conscious and treat itself as an adequate substitute for a traced-out curve.

minds; I speak also of ideas which we might verify if we would take the trouble, but which we hold for true although unterminated perceptually, because nothing says 'no' to us, and there is no contradicting truth in sight. To continue thinking unchallenged is, ninety-nine times out of a hundred, our practical substitute for knowing in the completed sense. As each experience runs by cognitive transition into the next one, and we nowhere feel a collision with what we elsewhere count as fact, we commit ourselves to the current as if the port were sure. We live, as it were, upon the front edge of an advancing wave-crest, and our sense of a determinate direction in falling forward is all we cover of the future of our path. It is as if a differential quotient should be conscious and treat itself as an adequate substitute for a traced-out curve. Our experience, *inter alia,* is of variations of rate and of direction, and lives in these transitions more than in the journey's end. The truncated experiences are sufficient to act upon — what more could we have *done* at those moments even if later verification were complete?

This is what, as a radical empiricist, I say to the charge that the objective reference which is so flagrant a character of our experiences involves a chasm and a mortal leap. A positively conjunctive transition involves neither chasm nor leap. Being the very original of what we mean by continuity, it makes a continuum wherever it appears. I know full well that such brief words as these will leave the hardened transcendentalist unshaken. Conjunctive experiences *separate* their terms, he will say: they are third things interposed, that have themselves to be conjoined by new links, and to invoke them makes our trouble infinitely worse. To 'feel' our motion forward is impossible. Motion implies terminus; and how can terminus be felt before we have arrived? The barest start and sally forwards, the barest tendency to leave the instant, involves the chasm and the leap. Conjunctive transitions are the most superficial of appearances, illusions of our sensibility which philosophical reflection pulverizes at a touch. Conception is our only trustworthy instrument, conception and the Absolute working hand in hand. Conception disintegrates experience utterly, but its disjunctions are easily overcome again when the Absolute takes up the task.

Such transcendentalists I must leave, provisionally at least, in full possession of their creed. I have no space for polemics in this article, so I shall simply formulate the empiricist doctrine as my hypothesis, leaving it to work or not work as it may.

Objective reference, I say then, is a mere incident of the fact that so much of our experience comes as an insufficient and is of process and transition. Our fields of experience have no more definite boundaries than have our fields of view. Both are fringed forever by a *more* that continuously develops, and that continuously supersedes them as life proceeds. The relations, generally speaking, are as real here as the terms are, and the only complaint of the transcendentalist's with which I could at all sympathize would be his charge that, by first making knowledge consist in external relations as I have done, and by then confessing that nine-tenths of the time these are not actually but only virtually there, I have knocked the solid bottom out of the whole business, and palmed off a mere substitute of knowledge for the genuine thing. Only the admission that our ideas are self-transcendent and 'true' already, in advance of the experiences that are to terminate them, can bring solidity back to knowledge in a world like this, in which transitions and terminations are only by exception carried out.

This seems to me an excellent place for applying the pragmatic method. When a dispute arises, that method consists in auguring what practical consequences would be different if one side rather than the other were true. If no difference can be thought of, the dispute is a quarrel over words.

What then would the *salto mortale* [mortal leap], the immediate self-transcendency affirmed as something existing independently of experiential mediation or termination, be known-as? What would it practically result in, were it true?

It could only result in our orientation, in the turning of our expectations and practical tendencies into the right path; and the right path here, so long as we and the object are not yet face to face (or can never get face to face, as in the case of ejects), would be the path that led us into the object's nearest neighborhood. Where direct acquaintance is lacking, 'knowledge about' is the next best thing, and an acquaintance with what actually lies about the object, and is most closely related to it, puts such knowledge within our grasp. Ether-waves and your anger, for example, are things in which my thoughts will never perceptually terminate, but my concepts of them lead me to their very brink, to the chromatic fringes and to the hurtful words and deeds which are their really next effects.

Even if our ideas did in themselves carry the postulated self-transcendency, it would still remain true that their putting us into possession of such effects *would be the sole cash-value of the self-transcendency for us.* And this cash-value, it is needless to say, is *verba-*

tim et literatim what our empiricist account pays in. On pragmatist principles, therefore, a dispute over self-transcendency here would be a pure logomachy. Call our concepts of ejective things self-transcendent or the reverse, it makes no difference, so long as we don't differ about the nature of that exalted virtue's fruits.

Fruits for us, humanistic fruits, of course. If an Absolute were proved to exist for other reasons, it might well appear that *his* knowledge is terminated in innumerable cases where ours is still incomplete. That, however, would be a fact indifferent to our knowledge. The latter would grow neither worse nor better, whether we acknowledged such an Absolute or left him out.

So the notion of a knowledge still *in transitu* and on its way joins hands here with that notion of a 'pure experience' which I tried to explain in my recent article entitled "Does 'Consciousness' Exist?" The instant field of the present is always experience in its 'pure' state, plain unqualified actuality, a simple *that*, as yet undifferentiated into thing and thought, and only virtually classifiable as objective fact or as some one's opinion about fact. This is as true when the field is conceptual as when it is perceptual. 'Memorial Hall' is 'there' in my idea as much as when I stand before it. I proceed to act on its account in either case. Only in the later experience that supersedes the present one is this *naïf* immediacy retrospectively split into two parts, a 'consciousness' and its 'content,' and the content corrected or confirmed. While still pure, or present, any experience — mine, for example, of what I write about in these very lines — passes for 'truth.' The morrow may reduce it to 'opinion.' The transcendentalist in all his particular knowledges is as liable to this reduction as I am: his Absolute does not save him. Why, then, need he quarrel with an account of knowing that merely leaves it liable to this inevitable condition? Why insist that knowing is a static relation out of time when it practically seems so much a function of our active life? For a thing to be valid, says Lotze, is the same as to make itself valid. When the whole universe seems only to be making itself valid and to be still incomplete (else why its ceaseless changing?) why, of all things, should knowing be exempt? Why should it not be making itself valid like everything else? That some parts of it may be already valid or verified beyond dispute, the empirical philosopher, of course, like any one else, may always hope.

VI. The Conterminousness of Different Minds

With transition and prospect thus enthroned in pure experience, it is impossible to subscribe to the idealism of the English school. Radical empiricism has, in fact, more affinities with natural realism than with the views of Berkeley or of Mill, and this can be easily shown.

For the Berkeleyan school, ideas (the verbal equivalent of what I term experiences) are discontinuous. The content of each is wholly immanent, and there are no transitions with which they are consubstantial and through which their beings may unite. Your Memorial Hall and mine, even when both are percepts, are wholly out of connection with each other. Our lives are a congeries of solipsisms, out of which in strict logic only a God could compose a universe even of discourse. No dynamic currents run between my objects and your objects. Never can our minds meet in the *same*.

The incredibility of such a philosophy is flagrant. It is 'cold, strained, and unnatural' in a supreme degree; and it may be doubted whether even Berkeley himself, who took it so religiously, really believed, when walking through the streets of London, that his spirit and the spirits of his fellow wayfarers had absolutely different towns in view.

To me the decisive reason in favor of our minds meeting in *some* common objects at least is that, unless I make that supposition, I have no motive for assuming that your mind exists at all. Why do I postulate your mind? Because I see your body acting in a certain way. Its gestures, facial movements, words and conduct generally, are 'expressive,' so I deem it actuated as my own is, by an inner life like mine. This argument from analogy is my *reason,* whether an instinctive belief runs before it or not. But what is 'your body' here but a percept in *my* field? It is only as animating *that* object, *my* object, that I have any occasion to think of you at all. If the body that you actuate be not the very body that I see there, but some duplicate body of your own with which that has nothing to do, we belong to different universes, you and I, and for me to speak of you is folly. Myriads of such universes even now may coexist, irrelevant to one another; my concern is solely with the universe with which my own life is connected.

In that perceptual part of my universe which I call your body, your mind and my mind meet and may be called conterminous. Your mind actuates that body and mine sees it; my thoughts pass into it as into their harmonious cognitive fulfilment; your emotions and volitions pass into it as causes into their effects.

But that percept hangs together with all our other physical percepts. They are of one stuff with it; and if it be our common possession, they must be so likewise. For instance, your hand lays hold of one end of a rope and my hand lays hold of the other end. We pull against each other. Can our two hands be mutual objects in this experience, and the rope not be mutual also? What is true of the rope is true of any other percept. Your objects are over and over again the same as mine. If I ask you *where* some object of yours is, our old Memorial Hall, for example, you point to *my* Memorial Hall with your *hand* which *I* see. If you alter an object in your world, put out a candle, for example, when I am present, *my* candle *ipso facto* goes out. It is only as altering my objects that I guess you to exist. If your objects do not coalesce with my objects, if they be not identically where mine are, they must be proved to be positively somewhere else. But no other location can be assigned for them, so their place must be what it seems to be, the same.*

Practically, then, our minds meet in a world of objects which they share in common, which would still be there, if one or several of the minds were destroyed. I can see no formal objection to this supposition's being literally true. On the principles which I am defending, a 'mind' or 'personal consciousness' is the name for a series of experiences run together by certain definite transitions, and an objective reality is a series of similar experiences knit by different transitions. If one and the same experience can figure

---

* The notion that our objects are inside of our respective heads is not seriously defensible, so I pass it by.

twice, once in a mental and once in a physical context (as I have tried, in my article on 'Consciousness,' to show that it can), one does not see why it might not figure thrice, or four times, or any number of times, by running into as many different mental contexts, just as the same point, lying at their intersection, can be continued into many different lines. Abolishing any number of contexts would not destroy the experience itself or its other contexts, any more than abolishing some of the point's linear continuations would destroy the others, or destroy the point itself.

I well know the subtle dialectic which insists that a term taken in another relation must needs be an intrinsically different term. The crux is always the old Greek one, that the same man can't be tall in relation to one neighbor, and short in relation to another, for that would make him tall and short at once. In this essay I can not stop to refute this dialectic, so I pass on, leaving my flank for the time exposed. But if my reader will only allow that the same *'now'* both ends his past and begins his future; or that, when he buys an acre of land from his neighbor, it is the same acre that successively figures in the two estates; or that when I pay him a dollar, the same dollar goes into his pocket that came out of mine; he will also in consistency have to allow that the same object may conceivably play a part in, as being related to the rest of, any number of otherwise entirely different minds.

This is enough for my present point: the common-sense notion of minds sharing the same object offers no special logical or epistemological difficulties of its own; it stands or falls with the general possibility of things being in conjunctive relation with other things at all.

In principle, then, let natural realism pass for possible. Your mind and mine *may* terminate in the same percept, not merely against it, as if it were a third external thing, but by inserting themselves into it and coalescing with it, for such is the sort of conjunctive union that appears to be experienced when a perceptual terminus 'fulfills.' Even so, two hawsers may embrace the same pile, and yet neither one of them touch any other part, except that pile, of what the other hawser is attached to.

It is therefore not a formal question, but a question of empirical fact solely, whether, when you and I are said to know the 'same' Memorial Hall, our minds do terminate at or in a numerically identical percept. Obviously, as a plain matter of fact, they do *not*. Apart from color-blindness and such possibilities, we see the Hall in different perspectives. You may be on one side of it and I on another. The percept of each of us, as he sees the surface of the Hall, is moreover only his provisional terminus. The next thing beyond my percept is not your mind, but more percepts of my own into which my first percept develops, the interior of the Hall, for instance, or the inner structure of its bricks and mortar. If our minds were in a literal sense *con*terminous, neither could get beyond the percept which they had in common, it would be an ultimate barrier between them — unless indeed they became 'co-conscious' over a still larger part of their content, which (thought-transference apart) is not supposed to be the actual case. In point of fact the ultimate common barrier can always be pushed, by both minds, farther than any actual percept, until at last it resolves itself into the mere notion of imperceptibles like atoms or ether, so that, where we do terminate in percepts, our knowledge is only speciously completed, being, in theoretic strictness, only a virtual knowledge of those remoter objects which conception carries out.

Is natural realism, permissible in logic, refuted then by empirical fact? Do our minds have no object in common after all?

Yes, they certainly have *Space* in common. On pragmatic principles we are obliged to predicate sameness wherever we can predicate no assignable point of difference. If two named things have every quality and function indiscernible, and are at the same time in the same place, they must be written down as numerically one thing under two different names. But there is no test discoverable, so far as I know, by which it can be shown that the place occupied by your percept of Memorial Hall differs from the place occupied by mine. The percepts themselves may be shown to differ; but if each of us be asked to point out where his percept is, we point to an identical spot. All the relations, whether geometrical or causal, of the Hall originate or terminate in that spot wherein our hands meet, and where each of us begins to work if he wishes to make the Hall change before the other's eyes. Just so it is with our bodies. That body of yours which you actuate and feel from within must be in the same spot as the body of yours which I see or touch from without. 'There' for me means where I place my finger. If you do not feel my finger's contact to be 'there' in *my* sense, when I place it on your body, where then do you feel it? Your inner actuations of your body also meet my finger *there:* it is *there* that you resist its push, or shrink back, or sweep the finger aside with your hand. Whatever farther knowledge either of us may acquire of the real constitution of the body which we thus feel, you from within and I from without, it is in that same place that the newly conceived or perceived constituents have to be located, and it is *through* that space that your and my mental intercourse with each other has always to be carried on, by the mediation of impressions which I convey thither, and of the reactions thence which those impressions may provoke from you.

In general terms, then, whatever differing contents our minds may eventually fill a place with, the place itself is a numerically identical content of the two minds, a piece of common property in which, through which, and over which they join. The receptacle of certain of our experiences being thus common, the experiences themselves might some day become common also. If that day ever did come, our thoughts would terminate in a complete empirical identity, there would be an end, so far as *those* experiences went, to our discussions about truth. No points of difference appearing, they would have to count as the same.

VII. Conclusion

With this we have the outlines of a philosophy of pure experience before us. At the outset of my essay, I called it a mosaic philosophy. In actual mosaics the pieces are held together by their bedding, for which bedding the Substances, transcendental Egos, or Absolutes of other philosophies may be taken to stand. In radical empiricism there is no bedding; it is as if the pieces clung together by their edges, the transitions experienced between them forming their cement. Of course such a metaphor is misleading, for in actual experience the more substantive and the more transitive parts run into each other continuously, there is in general no separateness needing to be

> ... one moment ... proliferates into the next by transitions which, whether conjunctive or disjunctive, continue the experiential tissue .... Life is in the transitions as much as in the terms connected.

overcome by an external cement; and whatever separateness is actually experienced is not overcome, it stays and counts as separateness to the end. But the metaphor serves to symbolize the fact that Experience itself, taken at large, can grow by its edges. That one moment of it proliferates into the next by transitions which, whether conjunctive or disjunctive, continue the experiential tissue, can not, I contend, be denied. Life is in the transitions as much as in the terms connected; often, indeed, it seems to be there more emphatically, as if our spurts and sallies forward were the real firing-line of the battle, were like the thin line of flame advancing across the dry autumnal field which the farmer proceeds to burn. In this line we live prospectively as well as retrospectively. It is 'of' the past, inasmuch as it comes expressly as the past's continuation; it is 'of' the future in so far as the future, when it comes, will have continued *it*.

These relations of continuous transition experienced are what make our experiences cognitive. In the simplest and completest cases the experiences are cognitive of one another. When one of them terminates a previous series of them with a sense of fulfilment, it, we say, is what those other experiences 'had in view.' The knowledge, in such a case, is verified; the truth is 'salted down.' Mainly, however, we live on speculative investments, or on our prospects only. But living on things *in posse* is as good as living in the actual, so long as our credit remains good. It is evident that for the most part it is good, and that the universe seldom protests our drafts.

In this sense we at every moment can continue to believe in an existing *beyond*. It is only in special cases that our confident rush forward gets rebuked. The beyond must, of course, always in our philosophy be itself of an experiential nature. If not a future experience of our own or a present one of our neighbor, it must be a thing in itself in Dr. Prince's and Professor Strong's sense of the term — that is, it must be an experience *for* itself whose relation to other things we translate into the action of molecules, ether-waves, or whatever else the physical symbols may be.* This opens the chapter of the relations of radical empiricism to panpsychism, into which I cannot enter now.

The beyond can in any case exist simultaneously — for it can be experienced *to have existed* simultaneously — with the experience that practically pos-

---

* Our minds and these ejective realities would still have space (or pseudo-space, as I believe Professor Strong calls the medium of interaction between 'things-in-themselves') in common. These would exist *where*, and begin to act *where*, we locate the molecules, etc., and *where* we perceive the sensible phenomena explained thereby.

tulates it by looking in its direction, or by turning or changing in the direction of which it is the goal. Pending that actuality of union, in the virtuality of which the 'truth,' even now, of the postulation consists, the beyond and its knower are entities split off from each other. The world is in so far forth a pluralism of which the unity is not fully experienced as yet. But, as fast as verifications come, trains of experience, once separate, run into one another; and that is why I said, earlier in my article, that the unity of the world is on the whole undergoing increase. The universe continually grows in quantity by new experiences that graft themselves upon the older mass; but these very new experiences often help the mass to a more consolidated form.

These are the main features of a philosophy of pure experience. It has innumerable other aspects and arouses innumerable questions, but the points I have touched on seem enough to make an entering wedge. In my own mind such a philosophy harmonizes best with a radical pluralism, with novelty and indeterminism, moralism and theism, and with the 'humanism' lately sprung upon us by the Oxford and the Chicago schools.* I can not, however, be sure that all these doctrines are its necessary and indispensable allies. It presents so many points of difference, both

* I have said something of this latter alliance in an article entitled "Humanism and Truth," in *Mind*, October, 1904.

from the common-sense and from the idealism that have made our philosophic language, that it is almost as difficult to state it as it is to think it out clearly, and if it is ever to grow into a respectable system, it will have to be built up by the contributions of many co-operating minds. It seems to me, as I said at the outset of this essay, that many minds are, in point of fact, now turning in a direction that points towards radical empiricism. If they are carried farther by my words, and if then they add their stronger voices to my feebler one, the publication of this essay will have been worth while.

VII.

Co-ordinate Matters of Immediate Feeling

by William James

from *"The Thing and Its Relations"*

'Pure experience' is the name which I gave to the immediate flux of life which furnishes the material to our later reflection with its conceptual categories. Only new-born babes, or men in semi-coma from sleep, drugs, illnesses, or blows, may be assumed to have an experience pure in the literal sense of a *that* which is not yet any definite *what*, tho ready to be all sorts of whats; full both of oneness and of manyness, but in respects that don't appear; changing throughout, yet so confusedly that its phases interpenetrate and no points, either of distinction or of identity, can be caught. Pure experience in this state is but another name for feeling or sensation. But the flux of it no sooner comes than it tends to fill itself with emphases, and these salient parts become identified and fixed and abstracted; so that experience now flows as if shot through with adjectives and nouns and prepositions and conjunctions. Its purity is only a relative term, meaning the proportional amount of unverbalized sensation which it still embodies.

Far back as we go, the flux, both as a whole and in its parts, is that of things conjunct and separated. The great continua of time, space, and the self envelope everything, betwixt them, and flow together without interfering. The things that they envelop come as separate in some ways and as continuous in others. Some sensations coalesce with some ideas, and others are irreconcilable. Qualities compenetrate one space, or exclude each other from it. They cling together persistently in groups that move as units, or else they separate. Their changes are abrupt or discontinuous; and their kinds resemble or differ; and, as they do so, they fall into either even or irregular series.

In all this the continuities and the discontinuities are absolutely co-ordinate matters of immediate feeling. The conjunctions are as primordial elements of 'fact' as are the distinctions and disjunctions. In the same act by which I feel that this passing minute is a new pulse of my life, I feel that the old life continues into it, and the feeling of continuance in no wise jars upon the simultaneous feeling of a novelty. They, too, compenetrate harmoniously. Prepositions, copulas, and conjunctions, 'is,' 'isn't,' 'then,' 'before,' 'in,' 'on,' 'beside,' 'between,' 'next,' 'like,' 'unlike,' 'as,' 'but,' flower out of the stream of pure experience, the stream of concretes or the sensational stream, as naturally as nouns and adjectives do, and they melt into it again as fluidly when we apply them to a new portion of the stream.

— *Essays in Radical Empiricism* (New York: Longmans, Green, 1912), pp. 93-95.

VIII.

Transitive tracts

from *The Principles of Psychology*

by William James

. . . difference in the rate of change lies at the basis
of a difference of subjective states of which we ought
immediately to speak. When the rate is slow we are
aware of the object of our thought in a comparatively
restful and stable way. When rapid, we are aware of
a passage, a relation, a transition *from* it, or *between*
it and something else. As we take, in fact, a general
view of the wonderful stream of our consciousness,
what strikes us first is this different pace of its parts.
Like a bird's life, it seems to be made of an alternation
of flights and perchings. The rhythm of language
expresses this, where every thought is expressed in
a sentence, and every sentence closed by a period.
The resting-places are usually occupied by sensorial
imaginations of some sort, whose peculiarity is that

they can be held before the mind for an indefinite time, and contemplated without changing; the places of flight are filled with thoughts of relations, static or dynamic, that for the most part obtain between the matters contemplated in the periods of comparative rest.

Let us call the resting-places the 'substantive parts,' and the places of flight the 'transitive parts,' of the stream of thought. It then appears that the main end of our thinking is at all times the attainment of some other substantive part than the one from which we have just been dislodged. And we may say that the main use of the transitive parts is to lead us from one substantive conclusion to another.

Now it is very difficult, introspectively, to see the transitive parts for what they really are. If they are but flights to a conclusion, stopping them to look at them before the conclusion is reached is really annihilating them. Whilst if we wait till the conclusion *be* reached, it so exceeds them in vigor and stability that it quite eclipses and swallows them up in its glare. Let anyone try to cut a thought across in the middle and get a look at its section, and he will see how difficult the introspective observation of the transitive tracts is. The rush of the thought is so headlong that it almost always brings us up at the conclusion before we can arrest it. Or if our purpose is nimble enough and we do arrest it, it ceases forthwith to be itself. As a snowflake caught in the warm hand is no longer a flake but a drop, so, instead of catching the feeling of relation moving to its term, we find we have caught some substantive thing, usually the last word we were pronouncing, statically taken, and with its function, tendency, and particular meaning in the sentence quite evaporated. The attempt at introspective analysis in these cases is in fact like seizing a spinning top to catch its motion, or trying to turn up the gas quickly enough to see how the darkness looks.

— *The Principles of Psychology* (Cambridge, MA: Harvard University Press, 1890/1983), pp. 236-237.

IX.

Like other revolutionary ideas, pure experience sciousness was mostly attacked in its own time. With some notable exceptions, such as Bergson, Dewey, and Whitehead, Western philosophers could not accept the reality, let alone the prime reality, of nondual experience. The resistance, though increasingly difficult to sustain, continues to this day.

The clearest understanding of sciousness, as it turned out, came not from a philosopher, but a Swiss psychologist, Theodore Flournoy, who was a mentor of Jung and a dear friend of James. A month before James died, he wrote to Flournoy that he wished he had lived closer to him so that he could have worked out some of his ideas in his company. For ". . . we seem," wrote James, "two men particularly well *faits pour nous comprendre.*" A year later, Flournoy published a book about James with the following chapter.

—J.B.

Radical Empiricism

by Theodore Flournoy

Let us now leave Pragmatism, which is compatible with many different systems, to take up the particular conceptions and more personal views with which it was associated in William James's mind. And at the outset let us place ourselves at the heart of this thinker's philosophy, at the very center from which the roads radiate in all directions. I refer to his Radical Empiricism or the doctrine of pure experience.

In order to grasp fully its originality, one must remember that in all ages philosophers have been divided between two opposing tendencies, rationalism and empiricism, according as they instinctively depended when seeking to discover reality, upon the mere use of reason or upon information derived from experience (external or internal), upon ideas or upon facts, upon the 'conceptual' or upon the 'perceptual.' We have seen that from the first James adhered to the second tendency, which is almost a racial heritage among Anglo-Saxon thinkers. But he believed that his predecessors had not known how to push their method to its conclusion, and that instead of deriving all that it was capable of yielding they had often forsaken it and fallen, like the rationalists, into the toils of vicious abstractionism. As against these inconsistent or short-winded empiricists, as well as against all rationalists, James presents his Radical Empiricism which makes reality coincide unqualifiedly with experience, and experience with reality. 'All that is experienced is real, and all that is real is experienced': such is the formula in which James might have summarized his doctrine had it not been for his aversion to propositions which seem to be dogmatic or absolute; and in so doing he would have excellently defined his empiricist position as in direct contrast with that Hegelian top notch of rationalism: 'All that is rational is real, and all that is real is rational.'

Let us survey briefly James's attitude in some of the principal branches of philosophy, that we may understand just how his empiricism goes further than that of his predecessors and so deserves the epithet *radical*, which he expressly prefixed to it.

I. First of all, in psychology, the most resolute empiricists, like Hume and John Stuart Mill, after having reduced our mental life introspectively to its elementary data (sensations of all sorts), have concluded from the fact of their *distinctness* for analysis that these elements are in reality originally *separate*, and have then found themselves unable to reconstruct the unity of our consciousness out of the dust of these isolated elements.* Thus they fell victim to their

. . . the soul is superfluous because the dilemma for which it was invented does not exist . . .

rationalist adversaries who have always declared the mysterious unity of the 'Ego' to be inexplicable save by a special metaphysical principle (the Soul, Monad, Spiritual Substance, Transcendental Apperception, etc.) adduced for the purpose of affecting the synthesis of this empirical multiplicity.

To this William James replies that the 'Soul' is a doubly useless hypothesis. First of all it is only a word substituted for an explanation, for if our consciousness were really composed of separate elements, one fails to see how one element more, a metaphysical entity beyond the field of direct observation, could succeed in reuniting them; the mystery is not to be solved by supposing behind the scenes a *deus ex machina* that shall somehow achieve the incomprehensible. But in the second place, more especially, the soul is superfluous because the dilemma for which it was invented does not exist; it is not true that our psychic life is made up of a multiplicity of elements, each having

* 'For my part,' said Hume, 'I must plead the privilege of a skeptic, and confess that this difficulty is too hard for my understanding' (*Treatise on Human Nature*, Book I, Appendix). And John Stuart Mill declared it 'inexplicable' and 'incomprehensible' that a succession of separate states of consciousness can take cognizance of itself, as a succession, in a new present state of consciousness. (*Examination of Sir William Hamilton's Philosophy*, Chapter XII)

its independent existence, which have to be reunited; for what actual experience presents is a multiplicity originally given *as one* act or *one* field of consciousness. The unity here is just as primitive as the multiplicity, and requires no more explanation than does the latter; the fact is sufficient. The one which is many, or the many which are one, is the plain empirical fact. In other words, it is altering the nature of reality to compare our consciousness, as does the whole empiricist school, to an aggregate, a mosaic of juxtaposed elements, as if to something like a cloud of dust or a shower of sparks. A simile which would better correspond to actual observation would be that of a continuous current, a stream in which the ripples succeed one another and pass continuously one into another without break. It is our abstract conceptual thought that, agreeably to its own disjunctive procedure, isolates and arbitrarily fixes certain portions of this stream of consciousness, taking no account of their real and continuous movement; just as instantaneous photography catches a galloping horse or a flying express-train and reports it in a motionless image on paper. But such an image is neither the train nor the horse, and the speed and power which in reality these possessed have all been lost. Such is the difference between our mental life as it is actually lived and this life as it is pictured in our descriptions and logical analyses.

For example, we conceive the present as a mathematical point or the blade of a knife, dividing the past which is no longer from the future which is not yet. But in the given reality these three things melt into one another without the least separation; every moment of our immediate experience is a becoming, a duration, which unites in an indivisible whole the future already dawning on the present and the present already moving into the past. Language with its separate words and logic with its static ideas are powerless to give a just account of this fluid, mobile reality, which to be rightly apprehended must be actually lived. Even in the cases where there appears to us to be a sudden break in continuity, resulting in the clear juxtaposition of two distinct states, — as when an unexpected explosion breaks in on silence, — if we observe carefully, we perceive that the first state continues into the second without, strictly speaking, any separation; and if we wish to describe the experience accurately we must admit that it was not the perception of an explosion but the perception-of-an-explosion-which-broke-the-silence. For the sense or the recollection of the preceding silence continues as an integral part of the perception of the noise.

To sum up, although every moment of our life, every pulsation of consciousness has for us a multiple content, a complexity of aspects or objects each of which our thought takes note of, and is so able to abstract it from the rest, this does not signify that such a moment of consciousness has been compounded from a collection of fragments whose synthesis must now be accounted for. Nor does it signify that our whole life is a series of separate moments which have to be strung together like the beads of a necklace upon a hidden metaphysical thread. In fact the continuity and unity of our consciousness or personality are immediately experienced, and are by this same token real. By carefully noting and describing this unity, James's radical empiricism guards against either losing sight of it, as does ordinary empiricism, or having to go for a so-called explanation of it to principles that are beyond the pale of experience, as does rationalism.

II. In epistemology (or the theory of knowledge) James's philosophy takes the same middle course between the two traditional extremes.

You know that in every cognitive act analysis discovers two factors, on the one hand the intuitions of sense or the data of perception, and on the other the intellectual elements which serve to bind the sense-intuitions together, such as the concepts of identity, resemblance, difference, space and time, quantity and quality, causality, finality, possibility, necessity, reality, and in short all the ideas of relation which are, so to speak, the skeleton of our thought, and the logical scaffolding of our scientific and philosophical edifices. Now empiricists have always been much embarrassed by these intellectual factors, for which they are unable to find a satisfactory origin among the sense-data; and so these factors straightway furnish the rationalists with an excuse for alleging that they are principles which utterly transcend experience. These are the rationalists' so-called innate ideas, *a priori* concepts, categories of the understanding, synthetic acts of pure reason, and so forth. Here again James takes his stand on introspective psychology and asserts that as a fact the relationships which our thought conceives as obtaining *between* the brute facts of sense, are themselves found just as much in immediate experience as are the brute facts!* The result is that the famous categories of the mind, which have always been the corner-stone of rationalism and the stumbling-block of classical empiricism, cease to exist for radical empiricism. For however transcen-

---

* James does not mean to imply that in each particular case the true relationships are necessarily perceived, for we should then be infallible; and should never be guilty, for example, of the famous sophism *post hoc ergo propter hoc* [after this, therefore because of this] which often leads us to admit a bond of causality where there is actually nothing but a chance succession. We are naturally subject to error and our experience must ceaselessly correct itself by extension and development; thus engendering science. What James means is that although we may be often deceived in experiencing these ideas of relation, nevertheless these ideas have their origin somehow in the immediate experience itself. For instance, our idea of causal connection is drawn from the undeniable experience of personal activity, yet we may still be in error when in special cases we seem to experience causality; just as when in a railway station we think that our own train is in motion while in reality it is the neighboring train, our illusion consists not in our belief in motion, which is perfectly real, but in our false localization of it.

dent and purely rational these concepts may appear to the superficial observation of the logicians, any careful psychologist can easily ascertain that they are wholly drawn from the facts of experience, and that their concrete reality is as undeniable as that of any other fact of experience. The truth is that our inner life is far richer, more varied and profound than most philosophers, whether empiricist or rationalist, have realized, and that when attentively examined it is found to contain a host of original experiences which have escaped the observation of both the one and the other.

This discovery, James's great contribution to psychology, constitutes the basis of his radical empiricism, both in metaphysics and epistemology. Before his time, phenomena were looked upon as sense-impressions only if their stability, and persistence in memory and imagination were sufficiently striking to attract the vulgar attention and to receive a name in the language, — such as red, cold, hard, mountain, table, joy, anger, and the like. And even in language there are many words, such as prepositions and conjunctions, which no one would have supposed to refer to a concretely felt or perceived entity; these are not, it was thought, facts of experience strictly speaking, but simply logical relations. Such words are *but, if, and, because, on condition that, then, for, neither, etc.* William James, in his celebrated essay 'On Some

Omissions of Introspective Psychology,' was the first to call attention to the fact that these words, however empty they may appear in themselves, are not without sensory content, and that each one of them, pronounced by itself, throws us into a mental attitude, an expectancy, sometimes almost an emotion, which is perfectly positive and distinct. Thus a definite sentiment is aroused by *but*, by *if*, by *where*, etc., — a sentiment which, though fleeting and unanalyzable, a mere transitive state between ideas where the mind as it were alights, is still as concretely precise, and actually *experienced* as are the most pronounced 'substantive states' (sensations, perceptions, images, and memories). It is true that in ordinary life we are too much absorbed by these latter, on account of their practical importance and their relative permanence, to notice the 'transitive states' which bind them together, and which are 'always on the wing, so to speak, and not to be glimpsed except in flight.' But just as the flight, in spite of its rapidity, is as much a fact as is the position of rest, so the quasi-instantaneousness of our passage from one mental state to another as we pronounce or hear pronounced the little connecting words in the course of a phrase, must not deceive us as to the positive and immediate reality of that experience of passage.

What I have just said in regard to those portions of consciousness which correspond to prepositions and conjunctions is only an illustration of these transitive states, which were entirely neglected until James established their full right to be recognized as psychic realities on a par with the substantive states. He adduces many other examples, which show us that these transitive states constitute the very threads of our life. They are those feelings of tendency, significance, intention, intellectual and moral attitude, those inner movements of all sorts which we so persistently name after the goals towards which they aim, that finally we come to notice only the latter and to lose sight of the equally real transitive process which leads up to them. If one applies oneself, as James did, and as contemporary psychology is doing more and more, to a consideration of these fleeting elements in our mental life, it becomes evident that the domain of what is directly experienced and lived extends far beyond the gross sensations which were all that had struck earlier observers. In the end this realm is found to be so far-reaching as to include everything, even the mental categories, so that in this continuous network constituted by the data of actual experience, there remains no gap through which to introduce elements of another order, such as the *a priori* principles of the rationalists.

III. There remains, however, one cardinal epistemological concept which seems to be exceptional in that it apparently cannot be traced back to experience, namely the idea of 'truth,' or the relation of consciousness to its object. Is it not, after all, the very essence of all consciousness that it has an object, that it points to something outside of and other than itself; and is it not evident that such a relation as that, the cognitive or noetic relation, is of a purely conceptual nature, quite foreign and irreducible to given facts of perceptual experience? These latter simply *are*, but do not aim at anything outside themselves. Are not the function of knowing and the idea of truth which is implied by it sufficient squarely to refute radical empiricism? This question occupied James a great deal. He studied it from every side and wrote a number of articles (afterwards collected in a book) whose object was to replace the intellectualist conception of truth, which he felt to be mere verbiage, by his own pragmatic conception, which is the only one that squares with the facts and with radical empiricism. Since this subject is somewhat intricate I shall try to illustrate James's idea by an elementary example.

While occupied at my desk I hear a noise outside the door and recognize the voice of my friend, Paul. Wherein consists the truth of my reflection, 'That is Paul'? The truth of this thought evidently lies in its conformity with its object, that is to say with the fact that it is indeed Paul, and no one else, who is in the vestibule. Unquestionably, replies the pragmatist, but what exactly does this vague word *conformity* (or its equivalents — correspondence, agreement, etc.) imply in this particular case?

In this case, many of you would doubtless answer, it signifies that if I should open the door I should actually find Paul; in other words I should see him, shake hands with him, speak to him, and thus directly ascertain that I had not been mistaken in thinking that I recognized his voice. Exactly so, James would reply. Your sound common sense leads you straight to the pragmatic definition of truth and, by the same token, to the verification of radical empiricism. The *truth* of my belief in Paul's presence lies in its verification by a series of concrete and immediate experiences: having heard Paul's voice I have risen from my chair, gone to the door of my room, opened it, entered the hall, seen, and fully verified the presence of my friend, Paul. In other words my initial experience (the hearing of Paul's voice) has led me, through a series of other clearly defined experiences, to my final experience which is the fulfillment of what the first one predicted.* And you clearly perceive that all this is but a succession of experiences, bound together by transitions that are equally experienced, and that nowhere are we dealing with any so-called purely con-

---

* For the sake of brevity I do not consider the case in which verification is completely followed out, and I omit James's theory of the conceptual substitutes for possible experience, with which we are so often satisfied.

ceptual relation between mind and a transcendent object.

But here the intellectualists will object: — You have just made the most unpardonable blunder, putting the cart before the horse and mistaking the effect for the cause. In point of fact it is not because your idea that Paul was outside was verified that it was true, but it is only because it was true that you were able to verify it. As for asking in what its truth, its conformity with its object, consists in *the particular case* that is simply a misconception; particular cases differ according to the nature of the thoughts and of their objects, but not in the relation that unites the one to the other, for it goes without saying that this relation — from the moment that it is what it should be, namely, truth and not error — is always the same, is universal, eternal, unique, and undefinable. It is, namely, the original relation called Truth! That truth is prior to all verification, and that it constitutes the inalienable essence of every 'true' proposition is self-evident, and must simply be acknowledged. What proof can you wish? Of the pair of contradictories, 'Mars is inhabited' and 'Mars is uninhabited,' we are taught by logic that one is necessarily true, the other false; and though it is doubtless to be regretted that we do not know which is true, that does not alter the case; the one that is true is so in and of itself, independently of any verification. And one may say that it always has been and always will be true. For even if the state of Mars were to change, that would in no way influence the eternal truth of the proposition expressing what it had been previous to that change. It is not even necessary that a proposition should be *thought* for it to be true; do you not know that among all the possible pairs of contradictory propositions, even among those which have never entered any one's mind and which perhaps never will, there is necessarily one of each pair that is true? And have not the scholastics already framed the concept of an Absolute Truth which comprises all these true propositions, and of which the partial truths that we discover are but the tiniest crumbs?

But the protestations of intellectualism do not mislead James. He sees but a verbal, abstractionist's chimera in this Platonic theory which makes of 'Truth' a sort of intermediate realm, prior to all human consciousness and hovering like some impalpable cloud between reality on the one hand and thought on the other. In his eyes these last two alone exist (both made, for that matter, of the same stuff — experience), and the term *truth* does not express any transcendent and indefinable relation to some sphere independent of ourselves, but it designates a particular relation, which always exists concretely, between the different portions of our experience itself. A state of consciousness, a bit of experience (such as hearing Paul's voice), is in itself neither true nor false; it *is*, merely, and bears the immediate evidence of its reality. But whether this initial state terminates through a series of concrete intermediaries (rising, going into the hall) in a new experience (the actual seeing of Paul) which is felt to be the continuation, development, and full confirmation of the first one; or whether, on the contrary, it terminates in a contradiction (finding myself in the presence of a stranger whose voice I had mistaken for Paul's): — it is in either case judged true or false retrospectively on the ground of an actual experience which of itself is in turn neither true nor false, but is what it is (the actual presence of Paul or of a stranger).* For James, in short, truth is not an intrinsic and indefinable quality of certain propositions, as it is for the intellectualists, but is something extrinsic and adventitious which adds itself to a fact of experience, and which consists in certain concrete relations supervening between this fact and the further course of experience.

As for the truths which have been handed down to us, such as that lead melts at 330°, that exercise insures health, that the square of the hypotenuse is equal . . ., etc. — these are summaries of past ex-

---

* This latter experience might in turn become retrospectively true or false in relation to some new and ulterior experience which should confirm or negate it (for instance, if I were to go on to recognize Paul's personal idiosyncrasies; or if I were suddenly to perceive that it was John who had disguised himself as Paul for a joke, etc.).

perience, desiccated formulae which spring into life only when they again actively take part at some particular juncture to guide our material or intellectual conduct; and then their truth consists, once more, in their practical success in leading us to new and satisfying experiences, which verify them afresh.

I cannot attempt to give you an adequate explanation, in so brief a compass, of the whole of James's doctrine of truth. What I have just said of it will suffice to give you a glimpse of the manner in which, by substituting the pragmatic for the intellectualist point of view, he makes the theory of knowledge harmonize with his radical empiricism.

IV. In metaphysics, finally, many who are loudest in proclaiming the method of experience still argue like pure rationalists when, in attempting to explain the world of phenomena, they imagine something else behind which serves as its substratum or support, some ultra-phenomenal or trans-experimental reality, an 'Absolute' hidden behind the 'Relative' — such as Spencer's Unknowable, Büchner's Force-matter, Haeckel's Substance, or, in the idealistic camp, Royce's God or Omniscient Thinker, etc. James's radical empiricism rejects all of these metaphysical principles as being quite as arbitrary and useless as the *'a priori'* is in epistemology or the 'Soul' in psychology.

In truth, not only do these fictions fail to furnish us with a precise explanation of a single phenomenon, since nothing concrete and particular can ever be deduced from them, but they lend a merely illusory support to the empirical world, which has no need for them and is sufficient in itself. Why pretend to support or fortify this world by a mysterious and inaccessible reality situated beyond, which in turn would require to be supported by another such, and so on to infinity: for where should we stop? Hindu mythology has the world resting upon an elephant, which rests upon a tortoise, which rests upon nothing; and since we inevitably reach this nothing, sooner or later, is it not more reasonable to suppress in the beginning the hypothetical tortoise and elephant and to recognize that the world of experience stands alone with no outside support? What childishness on the part of metaphysicians to wish to explain actual reality by means of a supposed reality, no idea of which latter can be obtained save by symbols borrowed from the former, which in itself should be accepted as simply an inexplicable fact. For as for furnishing a logical deduction of reality, or showing how being came from nothing, or establishing the necessity of the world or of God, we may as well give it up at the outset. We have today left far behind us the tricks of legerdemain by which Hegelian dialectic flattered itself that it accomplished this miracle. A sincere philosophy no longer attempts to unveil the manner in which that which exists sets to work to achieve existence; it accepts the reality already there, and proposes simply to study its details and character, but not to explain its presence, which will always remain a fact and for our thought an enigma. Why is there anything rather than nothing, and why is anything as it is rather than otherwise — these are questions that are susceptible of no answer; although that may not prevent their occurring to many a thinking mind. This being the case, James holds that serious philosophers must stick exclusively to the field of experience — ignoring, however, no part of this field — and that anything that does not form a part of it should be banished from discussion.*

After the considerations which I have just touched upon you will more easily understand the very concise outline in which James summed up his radical empiricism. It consists, according to him, of three points: first a postulate, next a statement of fact, and finally a generalized conclusion.

1. The postulate, on which he bases all discussion, is that 'the only things that shall be debatable among philosophers shall be things definable

---

* In order to be radical, he somewhere says, empiricism should admit in its constructions no element which has not been directly experienced, neither should it exclude any element that has been directly experienced.

in terms drawn from experience. (Things of an *un-experiencable* nature may exist *ad libitum*, but they form no part of the material for philosophic debate.)' This postulate eliminates at the outset from the field of discussion such metaphysical entities as the Unknowable, the Absolute, the Thing-in-itself, etc., which by definition are situated outside of all possible experience. In this James's radical empiricism agrees with the phenomenalism of Renouvier and of many modern thinkers, but it departs therefrom on the following point.

2. The statement of fact is that 'the relations between things, conjunctive as well as disjunctive (the connections as well as the separations), are just as much matters of direct particular experience, neither more so nor less so, than the things themselves.' This sums up what we have said above concerning the so-called categories of the mind, which it has been the custom to contrast with phenomena as elements of a different kind that hold the phenomena together. James ascertained that this difference of nature does not exist; what is conceptual is homogeneous with what is perceptual, ideas and things are 'consubstantial' — that is to say, are all made of the same stuff, namely, experience.

3. From the foregoing statement of fact James

derives the generalized conclusion, that all portions
of our phenomenal world are continuous one with
another, without any foreign principle being necessary to serve as their cement or support. 'The parts
of experience hold together from next to next by relations that are themselves parts of experience. The
directly apprehended universe needs, in short, no
extraneous trans-empirical connective support, but
possesses in its own right a concatenated or continuous structure.'

You see that the three elements into which James
divides his radical empiricism converge toward one
result, namely, to dispense with everything which is
not experienced. This amounts to having definitely exorcised from philosophy the fatal demon of the
'Absolute' which has so long possessed it and, like a
vampire, sucked its life blood; since in arrogating to
itself all true reality, it has left no reality for the empirical and temporal order of things, which is nevertheless both the setting and the substance of our
struggles, of our interests, efforts, and affections; in
short, of our whole practical and daily existence.

If you should ask me now for more detailed enlightenment as to the nature of this 'Experience'
which James substitutes as the true reality for the
traditional principles of the absolutist metaphysicians, for Matter, Substance, the Idea, etc.; or if you
should suspect it to be merely a new word substitut-

ed for the old ones; — I could only refer you to your-selves and to your own actual "experience," to let you verify it at firsthand. You will find there not, assur-edly, the whole reality of the universe, but at least a fair sample, a solid and authentic fragment of reality.

In this, James's empiricism is at the opposite pole from current metaphysics. Unquestionably experi-ence is a word — we cannot talk without words— just as Substance, Matter, Idea, etc.; but whereas these last expressions, in the mouths of their adepts, cover something prodigiously abstract, hidden, and distant, which we can attain only in thought or con-ceive only symbolically, experience or reality accord-ing to James designates primarily the most concrete, positive, immediate, and directly given thing that can possibly be; namely, our own present moment, our actual total *Erlebniss* [experience] just as we live it, in all its fullness and complexity. They mean at this moment, for instance, this hall with its heat and dazzling lights, the sensations arising from our in-ternal organs, the words which we utter or hear, the ideas and sentiments which they awake in us, the distractions which assail us, our more or less distinct sense of personality, of who and where we are, etc., etc. In ordinary life we frequently forget ourselves, and consider as real only the objects that particularly occupy us at the moment — flowers, curves of the second power, or the viands at a repast, according as